Restorative J[...]

M000168831

Learn how to implement a restorative justice approach that reduces suspension and expulsion rates, without compromising school safety and classroom order.

Author Dr. Zachary Scott Robbins, who has turned around schools in Boston, Massachusetts, and Las Vegas, Nevada, explores the assumptions that underpin school policies that lead to high rates of suspensions and expulsions, especially for African-American students. He shares his experiences using Restorative Justice Tribunals and Restorative Justice Circles, which strike an effective balance between serving consequences to students who misbehave and providing them with therapeutic wraparound supports.

This powerful book will help school leaders avoid discriminating based on race, national origin, or disability; will improve school climate; and will help teachers spend less time on discipline, so they can have more time for instruction and preparing students to graduate.

Zachary Scott Robbins is currently serving as a high school principal in Las Vegas, Nevada. Under his leadership, Zac's team established the first successful restorative justice program in Nevada, and his school functions as a training hub in restorative practices for Nevada educators. Prior to his work in Las Vegas, Zac was a high school principal in Boston in the city's most challenging school. Zac and his staff dramatically improved achievement, and the school was one of the most improved in the state. Follow him on Twitter and Instagram @DrZacRobbins.

Restorative Justice Tribunal

And Ways to Derail Jim Crow Discipline in Schools

Zachary Scott Robbins

Routledge
Taylor & Francis Group

NEW YORK AND LONDON

First published 2021
by Routledge
52 Vanderbilt Avenue, New York, NY 10017

and by Routledge
2 Park Square, Milton Park, Abingdon, Oxon, OX14 4RN

Routledge is an imprint of the Taylor & Francis Group, an informa business

© 2021 Zachary Scott Robbins

The right of Zachary Scott Robbins to be identified as author of
this work has been asserted by him in accordance with sections 77
and 78 of the Copyright, Designs and Patents Act 1988.

All rights reserved. No part of this book may be reprinted or
reproduced or utilised in any form or by any electronic,
mechanical, or other means, now known or hereafter invented,
including photocopying and recording, or in any information
storage or retrieval system, without permission in writing from
the publishers.

Trademark notice: Product or corporate names may be
trademarks or registered trademarks, and are used only for
identification and explanation without intent to infringe.

Some names have been changed to protect the privacy of individuals.

Library of Congress Cataloging-in-Publication Data
Names: Robbins, Zachary Scott, author.
Title: Restorative justice tribunal : and ways to derail Jim Crow
    discipline in schools / Zachary Scott Robbins.
Description: New York, NY : Routledge, 2021. | Includes
    bibliographical references. | Identifiers: LCCN 2020050596
    (print) | LCCN 2020050597 (ebook) | ISBN 9780367747756
    (hardback) | ISBN 9780367741440 (paperback) | ISBN
    9781003159506 (ebook)
Subjects: LCSH: School discipline—Untied States. | Behavior
    modification—United States. | Student suspension—
    Prevention—United States. | Student expulsion—
    Prevention—United Staes. | Restorative justice—United
    States. | African American youth—Education. |
    Discrimination in education—United States.
Classification: LCC LB3012.2 .R63 2021 (print) | LCC LB3012.2
    (ebook) | DDC 371.50973—dc23
LC record available at https://lccn.loc.gov/2020050596
LC ebook record available at https://lccn.loc.gov/2020050597

ISBN: 978-0-367-74775-6 (hbk)
ISBN: 978-0-367-74144-0 (pbk)
ISBN: 978-1-003-15950-6 (ebk)

Typeset in Palatino
by Apex CoVantage, LLC

Contents

Meet the Author

Dr. Zachary Scott Robbins is currently serving as a high school principal in Las Vegas, Nevada. Under his leadership, Zac's team established the first successful restorative justice program in Nevada, and his school functions as a training hub in restorative practices for Nevada educators. Prior to his work in Las Vegas, Zac was a high school principal in Boston in the city's most challenging school. Zac and his staff dramatically improved achievement, and the school was one of the most improved in the state. Zac completed his doctoral work at Boston College where he studied the relationship between racial identification, racial socialization, and how African-American students feel connected to schools and school-related outcomes. Zac has presented at both national and local conferences based on his work with restorative justice, cultural competency, whole-school transformations, and diversifying pipelines of teachers and leaders. Follow him on Twitter and Instagram @DrZacRobbins.

Preface

I was walking through McCarran International Airport in Las Vegas, Nevada, on my way to Hampton, Virginia, to see my mom who was having health complications. I was tired. Such is the life of a full-time high school principal and father of three small children living at home. What compounded my fatigue was worry. I was worried about my mom. My dad had been calling me with updates about my mom's health, and none of the updates were good. The bright spot in the middle of my fatigue was a sense of accomplishment at my school's restorative justice program's success. Things were working. We were reducing the suspensions of Black and brown students. Truth be told, I was too tired to enjoy the success and too busy to take a moment to celebrate it appropriately. That's not good, but it was what it was. This airport moment was happening right when my district was rolling out districtwide restorative justice efforts. But those efforts left me feeling disappointed. The restorative justice training my brother and sister principals received sometimes left them confused. They often contacted me to untangle and clarify what had been presented to them.

After dragging my carry-on bag through the airport for what seemed like an eternity, I collapsed into one of the uncomfortable airport chairs. That's when I received a phone call from Ms. Green, a school counselor, friend, and colleague you will meet in this book. "They trying to steal your stuff! They trying to take your ideas! Dr. Robbins, I'm telling you! They trying to claim your ideas as theirs!" Apparently, a group was developing some manual of disciplinary practices. When I saw a draft of the manual, it had so many creative thinkers' ideas in it, but none were given credit for their innovations. Included in the manual was a poorly written hodgepodge of components of the Restorative Justice Tribunal. Our ideas were in their manual, but no credit was given. It was wrong. In fact, it was shady.

Before I saw this manual, Ms. Green told me a local university professor kept asking her and Coach Esaw, another colleague of mine you'll meet in this book, for information about the Restorative Justice Tribunal. I made some inquiries about this inquisitive professor. I was told he was asking questions about the Tribunal as part of a program evaluation. That explanation seemed disingenuous. Was he evaluating a program or employees? Was he evaluating the district's restorative justice roll out, the outcomes from it, or both? Since little was standardized in the roll out of the district's approach, how would he make generalizations from outcome data? To tell me his inquiries were part of some sort of program evaluation seemed a little bootleg. That Thanksgiving holiday, I erupted words onto pages, and that work became the first draft of the book you have in your hands right now.

That following spring, legislators were beginning to prepare legislation to make restorative practices mandatory in Nevada schools. The late Nevada Assemblyman John Johnson was a champion of that legislation. I knew Assemblyman Johnson, but our relationship was purely professional. Ms. Green knew Assemblyman Johnson on a different level. They were less formal and prone to 'around the way' conversations. Ms. Green had already been talking with the Assemblyman about our situation, and she set up a conversation for the three of us. We talked with Assemblyman Johnson about our journey and challenges mobilizing restorative justice on a larger scale to help students, families, and schools. He listened to me tell the story about our restorative justice journey, and his response was simple and direct.

"Don't share anything else with them."

His plan was for us to tell our own story. We would testify about how we were using the Restorative Justice Tribunal to derail Jim Crow discipline during the upcoming legislative session. We would not be another group of African-American innovators to have their work co-opted and claimed by other people. He saw a benefit to my team and me training educators throughout the state. Unfortunately, Assemblyman Johnson passed away before we could mobilize the plan. His death shook the community to its core. We lost a good man and our champion in the legislature. He was such a good man that our school district named a school after him, and it was well deserved.

Restorative practices did become Nevada's law, but I did not tell our story at a legislative session. I'm going to tell you that story now. It's a remarkable story that will help students, their families, teachers, schools, and school districts.

For those folks who know me outside of these suits and alphabet-soup degree titles, let me say that a different way.

"Hey, we figured out how to keep kids in school. Let me holla' at you for a minute . . ."

1

Welcome to Your New School

Getting the Lay of the Land

Cheyenne High School has always been a school of historical importance to North Las Vegas. It was built, in part, in response to a failed court-mandated school integration plan. The court order addressed elementary schools, but the community was demanding more from the school district. New high schools were being built throughout the valley to keep up with Las Vegas' exploding population but none on the northside. After 42 years of waiting and after years of Black families watching their high schoolers get bused all over town to go to school, the school district built Cheyenne in 1991. Cheyenne was the pride of North Las Vegas and easily accessible to African-American students and families on the northside of town.

Unfortunately, Cheyenne has not enjoyed sustained academic success. Cheyenne has always been a tough school, residing in what became one of the most challenging areas in Las Vegas. Because a lot of the construction in North Las Vegas, like much of the Las Vegas Valley, is relatively new, poverty looks different. One may never suspect by looking at the homes and apartments around Cheyenne that the school resides in one of the oldest gang enclaves in the valley or that 90% of Cheyenne's students live in poverty. Gang activity sometimes spills over onto the school campus. The history of sustained underachievement and tough students heavily influences the narrative about teaching, learning, and working at Cheyenne.

Cheyenne's narrative of tough students and underachievement didn't sway my belief that all Cheyenne students could learn. My upbringing was similar to Cheyenne students'. Similar to my students' experiences, my family struggled financially. I remember being in the back seat of my dad's car, sandwiched between massive containers of water that we took to family members' homes when their water was shut off. My grandmother ran a 'shot house' to supplement her social security income. Shot houses are places where people illegally sold liquor to patrons. Things got rowdy in the shot house, and I remember going to grandma's living room window to watch grownups fight outside. My friends and I grew up conscious that gangs would jump any of us for looking at them the wrong way or saying something they deemed disrespectful.

While my students' experience in school was more heavily influenced by gangs and gang violence, my school experience was influenced more by racial tension. I grew up in Hampton, Virginia, and attended Francis Mallory Elementary School, which was named after a confederate naval officer. Next, I went to Jefferson Davis Junior High School, named after the president of the confederate states. Then, I graduated in 1990 from Bethel High School, which was named after the confederate army's Civil War battle of Big Bethel. The classes in these schools were tracked by ability level, and the faculties were predominately White. The historic attitudes toward Black people invoked by these schools' namesakes correlate with the academic expectations these faculties seemed to have of Black children. Many teachers did not expect superior academic performance from Black students.

My experience of growing up poor, immersed in an underground economy, and being unsupported by schools radicalized me. It radicalized me to ensure schools respond to all students' needs, regardless of students' families' financial situations or family circumstances. My fortune of earning college degrees and becoming a school principal inoculated me to any narrative that students were so hardened by life that they didn't value school. To me, the narrative of tough Cheyenne students who did not care about education or their futures was ridiculous.

When I first encountered staff members at Cheyenne, it was clear this narrative of hardened students who didn't care about school affected staff members' beliefs about Cheyenne students' potential. This belief influenced the degree that the staff pushed students to do the best work they could. While there were strikingly clear pockets of excellence in the school, Cheyenne High had devolved into a haven for horrific teaching where people with low expectations could find solace. I'll never forget the day one of my staff members—who was working to implement change—came into my office exasperated. That staff member was upset by a conversation she had with a highly respected 20-year veteran and influencer on staff who, reportedly, railed against programmatic changes occurring on campus. This attitude was despite a coalition of teacher leaders who supported whole-school improvement changes.

Reportedly, the 20-year veteran said, "I don't know why he's trying to get these kids to do so much. It's never going to work. They're never going to do it. I don't know what he thinks he's doing." The report confirmed several other accounts I had heard of this particular staff member being a 'hater.' After that year, this 20-year influencer transferred to another school, and the following year, Cheyenne's graduation rate and standardized test score pass rates soared to the best in the school's history. Of course, there is no causal relationship between those scores, graduation rates, and that staff member leaving, but it is ironic.

Viral Low Expectations

When I first took over as the principal of the school, my supervising administrator said, "Don't change anything," despite the school having low graduation rates and abysmal test scores. Of course, I didn't listen to that supervisor and did what I knew to be instructionally sound and what was right for the children.

A few weeks passed, and that supervisor called me in for a supervisory conference because several staff members complained that things were changing. Well, things were changing! The school had a 65% graduation rate. It had failed to provide students with a free and appropriate public education for years. During the supervisory meeting, my supervisor threatened to issue me a disciplinary 'write up' if I continued to make changes.

Shortly after the threat, two Caucasian assistant principals openly shared racially offensive thoughts about me, all within earshot of their support staff who were people of color. They said, "He only got his job because he's Black." They completely disregarded that the nearby middle school from which I had been promoted had the best achievement levels in that school's history.

At Cheyenne High School, teachers of students with exceptionalities routinely told families at Individualized Education Plan Meetings, "Don't worry about getting a regular diploma. You don't need a regular diploma to walk across the stage at graduation." They systematically convinced families of academically capable students with special needs that finishing high school with certificates of attendance rather than earning enough credits to earn a diploma was acceptable.

And the behavior management order of the day was to suspend, suspend, suspend, and expel students to maintain order. These were the things happening in the school I inherited. So much had to change.

As Challenges Resolved, New Problems Emerged

With prayer, networking, and a little luck, my supervisor retired, and that was the watershed moment that allowed me to start genuinely collaborating with staff to turn my school around. Based on the achievement of the years before I assumed leadership, Cheyenne was assigned a 'turnaround school' status. In my opinion, that designation was God working in mysterious ways. The turnaround status allowed me to transfer up to ten staff members out of the school at the end of every school year that my school had the turnaround designation. For three years in a row, I removed ineffective staff members. Many found jobs in different schools before I could ask the Human Resources Division to involuntarily transfer them to open job positions in other schools in the district. This benefit of the school turnaround process allowed Cheyenne to transform the definition of instructional excellence.

Over the next year, Cheyenne's graduation rate jumped from 65% to 78%. This climb was one of the most substantial increases in achievement for a high school in my school district's history during the standardized testing era. Soon after that, Nevada removed standardized testing as a condition for graduation, and our school's graduation rate increased to over 90%. The community began to reinvest in the school's success. Things were going well, but we still had a significant problem. Cheyenne High School was suspending and expelling African-American students five times more frequently than their Caucasian peers. Admittedly, that could be considered a trivial figure compared to other schools that were suspending African-American students seven to ten times more often than White students. Regardless, this was a problem.

Nationally, African-American boys and girls are suspended and expelled much more frequently than their peers of other races (Camera, 2020). However, Black males have particularly staggering disproportionate rates of out-of-school consequences. The Civil Rights Division of the Department of Justice rang the alarm on this problematic trend back in 2011 and again in 2014. The lack of policy change and inactivity of school leaders in addressing the matter suggests that it is a non-issue for many districts.

But the suspension rate at my school bothered me to my core. I was one of only three African-American principals at a comprehensive (mainstream) high school in the entire state of Nevada. There was no way in the world I could be a Black principal and be okay with continually jettisoning Black kids out of school. I felt that it would make me no better than school leaders who intentionally throw Black and brown kids out of schools.

Regardless of the district context regarding the suspensions and expulsions of African-American students, my 'house' wasn't in order. We were putting too many Black and brown kids out of school, and I couldn't have that on my conscience. I had to do something different.

I've never believed in store-bought programs or remedies, so for me, that was off the table as a solution. Then I investigated this approach to behavior management named 'restorative justice' working in the court system that some schools around the country were adopting.

My dissertation work had a substantial education psychology component to it, and I've always believed in therapeutic approaches to achieving long-term behavioral changes in students. Hence, the theoretical underpinnings of restorative justice intrigued me. At first glance, it seemed the way restorative practices operated in court systems would not work in my school. However, it was also clear that restorative practices could be molded into an approach that could help students and impact school climate in positive ways.

Reference

Camera, L. (2020, October 13). *School suspension data shows glaring disparities in discipline by race.* Retrieved from www.usnews.com/news/education-news/articles/2020-10-13/school-suspension-data-shows-glaring-disparities-in-discipline-by-race

2

Wading into Restorative Justice

Reflecting, Planning, and Getting My Mind Right

I remember sitting in my home office, wondering how I was going to launch restorative justice in a way that would stop African-American students from being suspended five times more frequently than their peers. To get my mind right about restorative justice (RJ), I read everything I could find on the subject. I read research studies, court documents, books, and magazine articles. I browsed the internet and read school districts' website accounts of how they rolled out restorative practices. I even read what companies and consultants that were selling RJ services to the public were pushing. Most of what I found focused on Restorative Justice Circles.

Origins for modern Restorative Justice Circles are rooted in New Zealand's Family Group Conferencing (Barn & Das, 2016).[1] Family Group Conferencing dates back to 1989, and it was a response to the disproportionate number of Maori children being removed by the court system from their homes and placed into state care. Family Group Conferences empowered participants to collaborate on solutions to concerns. In a majority of child welfare cases, Family Group Conferences had to occur before any court proceedings could begin. Family Group Conferences was essentially a diversion program.

Modern-era Restorative Justice Circles function similarly. The Circle brings people together to address behavior that has caused a 'harm' to someone in the community or to the community itself. The Circle typically has a facilitator who leads the discussion. Participants collaborate to understand a harm's impact on others. Before the Circle concludes, participants in the Circle agree on how to resolve the situation, repair the harm, and they evaluate the Circle process. Like the Family Group Conference model, Restorative Justice Circles divert students from out-of-school consequences.

After every article, report, or reflection I read about restorative justice, I arrived at the same conclusion. There was absolutely no way on earth restorative justice would work in my school if I did it in the way the literature was describing it. A lot of what I read about restorative justice chronicled how RJ worked in the criminal justice system. This made sense because restorative justice has roots in the criminal justice system ("RJ in the Criminal Justice System"). However, many aspects of the criminal justice system models of restorative justice could not work in my school. We couldn't compel offenders to participate in restorative justice like the courts could, so that approach wasn't going to work. In the court system, a restorative justice court judge can mandate that an offender attend counseling, drug treatment, or pay restitution, along with any other actions the court accepted in a restorative agreement to repair a harm. Courts have these options and wraparound services available to them. Most schools don't. Mine definitely didn't. We did not have a phalanx of school psychologists or social workers available to students or their families. Also, offenders in the court systems are motivated to honor their restorative agreements in order to avoid jail time and to have their criminal cases dismissed. While avoiding out-of-school consequences can motivate students and families to participate in school-based restorative justice, participating in restorative justice to avoid a suspension or expulsion is hardly the same as participating to avoid jail time or a criminal record. Thus, I did not feel the justice system brand of restorative justice would work in my school.

I also felt it would not be wise to ask teachers to pause classes to run a Restorative Justice Circle every time a student misbehaved in class. Even if teachers could become skilled enough (quickly enough) to effectively facilitate Restorative Circles, the disruptions to learning would be too numerous. I also could not ignore the fact that some of the students in my school terrified their teachers. It just was what it was. It is one thing to hear stories about students who are hardened by life or to see caricatures of them on television. It was an entirely different experience for teachers to work with the fictitious caricatures' real-life embodiments. Some of my students were fearless, could care less about adult authority, and only responded to teachers' reasonable requests if teachers spoke to them in certain ways. Some of my students responded viscerally and aggressively when they felt teachers were 'out of line' in how they attempted to maintain order. When students felt their teachers crossed a line, were disrespectful, or embarrassed them, students sometimes cursed their teachers out or (on rare occasions) threatened to harm them physically. I felt it would be unreasonable for me to expect these teachers to have—or even slowly develop—the skills to run Circles in their classes after turbulent moments with these students.

In the classroom, every moment counts. The moments count even more when students enter school multiple grade levels behind in their academic proficiency, like most of my students. My performance evaluation is based—tangentially—on how students perform on the American College Testing (ACT) and Advanced Placement exams. Students' credit sufficiency also factors into my performance evaluation, as it should. I needed teachers to maximize every instructional minute available to students. It would have been crazy for me to ask my staff to stop school (somewhat frequently) to run Restorative Justice Circles.

In addition to the problem of stopping school to run Circles, every teacher, while they may love children, may not be well-equipped to provide mentorship and guidance to students over and above their normal teaching responsibilities. I remember dealing with this challenge as an assistant principal when a school where I worked launched a whole-school advisory program. The advisory program was not as effective as it probably could have been because some of our advisory teachers did not have the disposition to advise and mentor students. We created an advisory curriculum, and advisory groups met regularly. We facilitated training, and teachers checked in on students' academic progress and emotional well-being. The disparity of students' engagement among advisory groups was strikingly noticeable. Some of the advisory program teachers had difficulty developing the trust and relationships with students that make advisory periods rich. These teachers were good people and fantastic content-area teachers. They just weren't great advisory teachers. Because we launched advisory with only six teachers, we made it work. Upon reflection, I don't know how much positive impact the advisory program would have had if we required every teacher on staff to be an advisor. I'm glad we didn't.

That experience of launching advisory was instructive for my plans to launch restorative justice at my school. I decided that I would not launch a restorative justice effort that used teacher-led Circles as the primary mode of intervention. Several reports on schools' roll out of restorative practices concluded that teachers needed more training in Restorative Circles (Augustine et al., 2018). In those program evaluations I read, lack of training led teachers to feel that restorative practices were not effective. Researchers in those program evaluations concurred. Because of my experience rolling out whole-school advisory, I wonder the degree to which those programs evaluations would have changed if the teachers in those evaluated schools received more training. I wonder how much more training would have helped. Yes, I believe in the growth mindset. Yes, I believe that employees can pick up skills with proper training. I still maintain that some people are more predisposed than others to influence students' behavior through discussion. I didn't think mandating that teachers be mentors was the right answer for that advisory program back in the day. And I don't believe mandating that all teachers run Restorative Circles is a good idea now. This is what is happening in many schools implementing restorative practices.

In addition to my concerns with mandatory Restorative Circles, the schools regarded as restorative justice models didn't appear to be like my school. The schools where restorative justice studies took place didn't have almost 200 people on their teaching staff. The researchers didn't describe neighborhoods that were mortally dangerous and where that danger impacted teaching and learning on campus. I didn't see my school or myself or my staff's challenges in much of the literature. I didn't see in the literature descriptions of classroom environments that at times became frenetically turbulent, tough students, and discussions of teacher turnover. Teachers and administrators in my school could earn the same salaries in other schools in our district and encounter far fewer challenges. But something had to be done at Cheyenne. We could not keep doing what we were doing, given Black students' suspension and expulsion rates.

In the midst of all of the roles and responsibilities of running a school, I began to reflect on how a restorative justice program might look at Cheyenne. I put together an outline of an approach that later became the Restorative Justice Tribunal. The best vision is a shared vision, and I knew that whatever approach I put in place would not work unless I got input from students.

A Tailored Restorative Solution for Unique Students

I wasn't arrogant enough to believe that a restorative justice program would work well without input and guidance from my students. Their perspectives, life experiences, social norms, and the hardships they navigate are unique. Ninety percent of students in my school live in poverty. While I don't believe in painting with a broad brush or making sweeping generalizations, it isn't too much of a stretch for me to say that many of my students live hard lives. Some of the most respectful, genuinely nice students go to great lengths to help their families keep food on their tables and stay safe.

Some of the nicest, kindest students in my school hold the doors open for female teachers. They ask lost visitors if they need help finding locations on campus during the day. Some of these same wonderfully nice students put bullets in their enemies at night. Some of our most promising scholars take multiple advanced placements or dual enrollment courses during the day. At night, they go home to care for several siblings while their parents work multiple jobs to pay bills. This is a typical arrangement in a 24-hour town like Las Vegas. I've had female students move out of their homes to escape human trafficking. And it's only been the cases where police detectives got involved that we were able to help them. Other cases go under the radar.

As I've previously stated, my school resides in one of the oldest African-American gang enclaves in the Las Vegas Valley. The neighborhood is unique. One thing I learned from working in the neighborhood for over ten years is old-school child-rearing rules applied. This was comforting to me because the rules were familiar to me. It was (and still is) a cardinal sin for a kid to do something that prompted the school to call their parents at their job. This rule was (and still is) especially true in Las Vegas because casinos do not take interruptions to employees' work shifts lightly. If I (as the principal) called a student's family, the family typically worked in partnership with the school no matter the level of dysfunction (if any) occurring in that student's home.

I'm proud that an overwhelming majority of our parents partner with us to help their students learn. But there is a small population of our parents who behave unpredictably. These parents who work earnestly with us to help their kids succeed would sometimes come to our campus to fight other people's children or to fight each other. They would challenge each other on social media and meet in the parking lot to fight. Instances of these rumbles have decreased over the years but occur occasionally.

This is our normal. Our student population was unique, indeed. I needed a unique solution to exceptional circumstances, so I wasn't buying what the restorative justice experts at that time were selling. I needed a unique solution to reduce suspensions, expulsions, and overall conflicts on campus, something other than prompting teachers to situate their students in a circle and pass around a talking piece. That method wasn't going to work, even if the same aim applied. To be clear, I had a goal to reduce suspensions and get participants to see how their actions impacted the entire community. I also had to encourage them to make restoration before the restorative intervention concluded. We had to succeed. We just had to because so much was at stake for our students and school. I was done with my school and its students being doubted and disregarded due to Cheyenne's historic underachievement. I was done with the automatic assumption that our school and students weren't worthy of care and concern because of the few bad actors that affirmed the toughness of our school and neighborhood. I was done with my teachers not getting respect from their peers when they consistently catapulted the achievement of students who entered my school several grade levels behind in math and reading. Students on suspension don't learn as much as students sitting in classes. None of these perceptions would change until we reduced disproportionate suspensions and expulsions and kept more students in school. If we failed, it would ultimately be my failure. I was the principal, the 'principal/principle' teacher of my school.

Don't Proceed Without Students' Input

I sought out students' insight about essential conceptual elements of restorative justice before beginning. Aside from my general belief that students should be partners in school governance, I knew their input would be illuminating. This was particularly true because the school-based programs I'd researched were mostly found in small schools, suburban schools, or were designed for small numbers of student offenders. The school-based programs in urban schools, I found, were more like youth court of conflict mediation training. Because of my students' wariness of the police and legal system, I knew that youth court was not the right approach. I didn't want to ask students to choose to identify with a legal system that so many of them didn't trust. I did not think mediation training should be a cornerstone of our solution to reducing suspensions and expulsions. Conflicts in my school were unpredictable and volatile, so I didn't want to risk students being pulled into conflicts that evolved into out-of-school neighborhood beef between groups of students.

I was not finding the solution I needed to reduce suspensions and expulsions and change school culture. Ultimately, I started with what I had. I found a book online about restorative justice, but it was primarily for the court system. The book was free to the public and written well enough. It would have to do. I went through the book and removed the sections written specifically for the court system.

Next, I asked one AP Seminar class and one AP English Literature class to read the book. I asked them to tell me what they felt were the most critical elements of an effective restorative justice approach. Resoundingly, the students said any restorative justice approach that was going to work at Cheyenne had to allow students to be 'genuinely' heard. Specifically, my students said they wanted their teachers to hear their side of the story whenever they got in trouble for making a bad choice. This was regardless of if they felt students deserved a disciplinary response or not.

After reading the research on restorative justice, the students also said they thought it was important that offenders understood how they fit into the whole of the school community. This was also incredibly unique because it is a survival strategy in our school for students to project an air of being aloof. This idea would evolve into an aspect of my approach to facilitating the Restorative Justice Tribunal that is remarkably counterintuitive. In a place where kids insisted on projecting indifference as a strategy to survive, they said the restorative justice approach had to help them recognize their place among the whole of the community. In alignment with this thinking, the students shared that their peers do not understand how their actions—specifically misbehaviors—impact the broader school community.

While I suspected some of what the students might say, what they expressed was exactly what I needed to know. The thoughts they shared became the procedural foundation of the restorative justice solution I ultimately put in place. I had to figure out a way to reduce suspensions and expulsions of our African-American students. To do this, I needed to create a workflow that allowed students to tell their stories, be heard by their teachers, and help students understand how their behaviors impacted others. These became the waypoints on the road map for Cheyenne High School's restorative justice solution.

After implementing our restorative justice solution (the Restorative Justice Tribunal), we achieved a 98% success rate. In our first year, we heard 434 restorative justice cases. Only five cases had to be referred back to the Deans' Office because offenders refused to participate or misbehaved while in restorative justice structures. Students who went through our restorative justice program didn't get referred repeatedly for misbehaving in school. They were not committing more serious behavior infractions. More students were behaving and seeing the importance of righting their wrongs in the school community. One thing offenders had to do was apologize to their class if they disrupted learning. It was not enough to simply stand in front of the class and say, "I'm sorry." Offenders had to write a meaningful apology letter that was vetted by Restorative Justice Tribunal facilitators. Offenders had to read those letters to their class and teacher.

I remember one day, shortly after we started running Tribunals, several of Cheyenne High School's assistant principals were off campus, so Ms. Green, the school counselor and a restorative justice facilitator, asked me to accompany her to take a student to read an apology letter to her class. The student's name was Elsa. As Ms. Green and I accompanied Elsa to read her apology letter to her class, I made small talk with her. By that point of the Restorative Justice Tribunal process, offenders would have done much guided and personal reflection on their behavior. There was no need for me to pile on or browbeat them about a poor behavior choice. Besides, casual talk allowed me to deepen my relationships with students on campus.

Elsa was as admirable as she was tough. She projected a bulletproof toughness as we talked and walked to the classroom. Elsa's strength was impenetrable until we got to the classroom door. That's when the tough exterior melted, and she became a vulnerable young student, nervous about being in front of her peers. It was also clear that she genuinely felt bad about being disruptive. Dare I say, Elsa felt ashamed.

Ms. Green asked the teacher if she could interrupt the class for a moment. Then Ms. Green announced that one of their peers had something she would like to say to them and to please give her their respect and undivided attention. Elsa read her apology letter with a shaky voice. In fact, her whole body shook, and the paper trembled in her hand. When she finished reading her apology letter, the class applauded her. They were 'with' her, and I'm sure many saw their personal struggles in Elsa and experienced catharsis through hers.

Her teacher said, "We accept your apology. Welcome." Elsa went to her seat. The teacher kept teaching, and learning continued.

While walking back to my office, I turned to Ms. Green and said, "This is going to work."

Ms. Green turned, smiled, and said, "It's already working, Dr. Robbins."

We were onto something. The Restorative Justice Tribunal was reducing out-of-school consequences. Somehow I needed to expand the restorative justice program's reach. Also, I had to figure out how to pay for it all during a time when teachers were upset over their teaching contracts and collective bargaining negotiations for pay increases.

Note

1. https://chicago.suntimes.com/2020/8/7/21357874/restorative-courts-expanding-chicago-tim-evans-cook-county-justice-system, https://academic.oup.com/bjsw/article/46/4/942/2472186

Further Reading

Augustine, C. H., Engberg, J., Grimm, G. E., Lee, E., Wang, E. L., Christianson, K., & Joseph, A. A. (2018). Can restorative practices improve school climate and curb suspensions? In *An evaluation of the impact of restorative practices in a mid-sized urban school district*. Santa Monica, CA: Rand.

Barn, R., & Das, C. (2016). Family group conferences and cultural competence in social work. *The British Journal of Social Work, 46*(4), 942–959.

RJ in the criminal justice system. Retrieved from http://restorativejustice.org/restorative-justice/rj-in-the-criminal-justice-system/

3

Financing the Restorative Justice Tribunal

I Went Begging for Money

When it was time to launch the Restorative Justice Tribunal, my district experienced one of the most significant budget crises in its history. The district had already cut funding to special education, summer school, the central office, school police services, and the English Language Learner Division. It had also forced schools to cut funding from their budgets, which affected personnel and school supplies. The cuts totaled roughly 50 million dollars, and one of the proposed solutions was a continued salary freeze for employees.

What nobody knew at that time was the cut would be the first of several budget cuts that ultimately led to an ugly standoff between the teachers' union and the school district. This situation required the Governor's intervention to get resolved. This was the backdrop for the launch of restorative justice at my school. Budget cuts, salary freezes, media outlets claiming a lack of fiscal accountability, and whispers of a teacher strike if things didn't change for the better.

Teachers were fed up with being underpaid, and districts throughout the state were lobbying legislatures to dole up more dough for education, with good reason. At the printing of this book, Nevada's school funding formula is unconscionably inadequate. At the same time, Nevada's per-pupil funding formula is among the lowest in the United States ("Comparing per-pupil funding from 1960 to 2019 misses the big picture," 2019). To be fair, also at the printing of this book, Nevada's legislature had passed legislation to remedy some of the funding challenges. The State was working toward a more systemic solution to Nevada's school funding woes.

I knew restorative justice had a tough hill to climb. The fiscal climate in my district would not be friendly to anything perceived as non-essential. We already had a hard road to travel because suspensions and expulsions were the tools my school community preferred to use to maintain order. They were used to assign value to classroom learning and to ensure school safety. Quite frankly, to a certain degree that was working. Suspension and expulsion were also the tools used to compensate for a lack of professional skills. Some teachers who lacked classroom management skills were unwilling to form relationships with students, and/or they were unable to be mindful of how their implicit biases affected power relationships between them and their students.

For some in my school, suspensions and expulsion were used to enforce oppressive Jim Crow disciplinary structures. I'll discuss Jim Crow discipline in more detail later.

I knew the mere mention of reducing suspensions and expulsions at my school would be met with resistance. For the faculty and staff, it would be a change from the cultural norm. Also, the changes would require the workforce—already frustrated from feeling underpaid and overworked—to do more. I was trying to address a problem that most of the faculty did not perceive as a problem—rather, they saw it as a benefit. So, spending money to add a staff member to our overstretched budget would add to their resistance. If I did not find a means of paying for my school's restorative justice program outside of our regular school budget, I doubted the program would get off the ground. I could start the program, despite the budget crisis, through edict, direction, or through brute force. But if I did, the resistance and dislike for the restorative justice program would most likely be insurmountable.

The budget woes of the district required me to cut positions to balance our school budget. The decision to cut a job is ultimately a fiscal decision. It typically costs schools several thousand dollars to run each class period of a course. If a teacher has a full class, that class is a good return on the investment of the public's dollars. If a teacher's class is half full for no good reason, there is no fiscally responsible reason to continue to offer the course. Sometimes, there are good reasons for a school to run small courses, like in the instance of enrichment courses for students who need academic support. The classes are expensive but worth the cost.

As most school leaders are hesitant to cut core, required courses, principals typically look (unfortunately) at elective classes as the first place to cut staff during tough fiscal times. The other place that school leaders look at is career and technical education elective courses, particularly, those that are no longer supported by state funding or that have been removed from the state's list of 'critical job shortage' areas. Removed programs are those that will soon stop receiving state funding for materials, supplies, and even salaries. If a teacher's elective course is not full, they are prime candidates to be cut during a fiscal crisis.

In 2014–2015, the school year I launched restorative justice, I was cutting a few elective teachers, some of whom happened to be heavily involved in our district's teachers' union. Some were vocal union supporters. As difficult personally as it was for me to cut staff, our circumstances were dictated by the budget woes. Thankfully, the staff I cut were not out of a job. They were involuntarily transferred by the district to open positions in other schools. Even after those cuts, I still didn't have enough dough to run the school adequately. I had cut out of our school budget anything that anyone could perceive as fat. Cutting anything else would have meant cutting into bones.

I was at a point where I could not cut any more personnel from our budget and still be able to schedule classes for all of our students. Yet, I had to find a way to fund a position to address disproportionate suspensions and expulsions. In my preliminary plan for the Restorative Justice Tribunal, I needed another school counselor to pull it off. I couldn't reduce the workload of one of our existing school counselors so that she could facilitate restorative justice. In that scenario, her colleagues would have to take the students from her caseload, along with all of her counseling responsibilities. That would not have been fair and would have been received poorly. The licensed personnel were already feeling overworked and underpaid.

It was clear that I needed more money for my school. I needed enough dough for another position on my staff to implement the Restorative Justice Tribunal. I went begging for money, and luck was on my side.

The Local Climate and Appetite for Change

The Civil Rights Division of the United States Department of Justice had been 'looking into' districts disproportionately suspending and expelling students of color. Mine was one of them.

This was not a club that school districts wanted to be a part of. A bunch of school districts across the country had received 'watch your back' letters from the Department of Justice. In my opinion, being put on notice was a good thing. It was much better than being the subject of an adverse action led by the Feds. The Civil Rights Division of the Department of Justice was telling school districts that the Department knew something was wrong with their disciplinary practices. This notice gave the districts time to get their houses in order. The Clark County School District, where I worked, was one such district whose suspension and expulsion practices the Department of Justice was observing. And that was the leverage I used to beg for money.

I'll never forget the day. Our district brought in a consultancy group to facilitate a summer training forum. The purpose of the training was to help solve the puzzle of why our alternative

education schools were not having a greater return on investment. The reoffending rate of students at our 'behavior schools'
was high. The training was designed to, among other things,
help schools engage with students in ways that prevented them
from being referred to alternative schools. I sent my staff to the
training as directed. About an hour into the training, I got text
messages from them expressing displeasure about the training.
As the text messages increased in frequency, I got dressed to
pop in on the training. I didn't live far from where it was taking
place. I needed to find my staff members so they could air their
frustrations about the presentation directly to me, have their
frustrations heard, and then reengage.

Also, I needed to find the district leader whose office spon-
sored the training and beg her for money. I highly suspected
the big boss allocated an astronomical amount of money—either
from a grant or from the general fund—for the training because
professional development for so many people is expensive.

I found the big boss, and I asked for a much smaller amount
of money. I asked for one paid position. That's it. I had a few
things going for me in the conversation, so in terms of my timing,
I was lucky. Restorative Justice was a new and shiny concept. It
was the new 'thing.' People gravitate toward new and shiny things.
I explained that I had done my research, and I passionately laid
my research out for her. I had a reputation in the district for trying
innovative things. This standing came from my history; I had just
turned around a middle school that nobody thought could succeed, in part from implementing a series of innovations.

I shared that I had arranged to take my team to a restorative
justice conference as I wanted the approach I was developing
to be informed by current trends and thinking. My extensive
research meant that I had a broader background knowledge than
others in the district. In addition, I thought differently about the
problem of disproportionate suspensions and expulsions and
the urgency of finding a solution. The district leader was also
aware that I had already participated in a districtwide task force
to reduce suspensions and expulsions. The committee was called
The Superintendent's Educational Opportunities Advisory
Council II, and its role was to provide policy recommendations

to the superintendent (in 2013). The Council's focus was to address the fact that African-American students accounted for 43% of all high school student expulsions at that time. This rate was despite African-American students comprising only 12% of the student population of the district.

Ironically, our Council recommended that the district provide cultural competency training, provide early intervention to students who frequently display behavior difficulties, and provide better alternatives to suspension and expulsion as well as monitor progress (Council, 2013). All of these recommendations will be discussed in this book. The Restorative Justice Tribunal model synthesizes all of these policy recommendations in a comprehensive, easily replicated approach for any school or school district.

Another factor in favor of my request was that the money I was asking for was peanuts, especially compared to what was just spent on the consultants facilitating the training. Ultimately, she authorized the money for the position I requested. My begging worked!

Were it not for her, I do not know if the Restorative Justice Tribunal would have launched that year. I am so appreciative that she had the faith to let me try a different approach to reducing suspensions and expulsions. I know for a fact that she was fighting battles far above my pay grade that nobody saw and that few of us would have understood at that time. She could have denied my request, but she didn't. I'm so grateful to her for that. I had no idea that decision would lead to the success the Restorative Justice Tribunal would have.

References

Comparing per-pupil funding from 1960 to 2019 misses the big picture. (2019, October 25). Retrieved from https://lasvegassun.com/news/2019/oct/25/comparing-per-pupil-funding-from-1960-to-2019-miss/

Council, S. S. E. O. A. (2013). *Final report on overrepresentation by gender, race/ethnicity, or disability in discipline-related actions and/or special education placement.* Las Vegas. Retrieved from https://secure.ccsd.net/internal/cms/doc-vault/resources/archive/final-seoac-recommendations-report.pdf

4

Structures to Ensure a Return on Investment

Remove Structural Barriers

After getting the dough for the counselor position, I had to make sure we got a return on the investment of that dough. I examined various policies and structures influencing suspensions and expulsions in our school, including our school's relationship with on-site school police officers.

Zero tolerance is a structural barrier to keeping students in school and away from unnecessary out-of-school consequences because it is policy that has been contorted into Jim Crow discipline. Zero-tolerance policies were designed to maintain school safety when students committed egregious acts, such as bringing weapons or controlled substances to school. Our school was not a zero-tolerance school because our district wasn't a zero-tolerance district. This means that we did not expel students from school unless they committed these most serious behavioral offenses. Historically, zero-tolerance policies have been used to provide pathways for excessive punishment when students misbehave in relatively benign ways. It appears students' journeys to suspension and expulsion have sometimes been accelerated by teachers' (sometimes unconscious) bias toward behaviors they sometimes perceive as cultural deficiencies in students. They use out-of-school consequences as the tool to extinguish those behaviors, and zero-tolerance policies have paved the way for that to happen.

Zero-tolerance policies were originally designed to address the problem of rising violence and weapons in schools. On the face of it, the policies and their intent make sense. It is not in the public's interest to tolerate students bringing weapons to school. No parent should have to worry if their school or school district will do all it can to stop students from bringing weapons onto school campuses. Upon analysis of the suspension and expulsion rates of students of color, particularly of African-American students, it appears that these discipline policies and procedures are what needs to be addressed. If the disproportionate application of discipline policies is not the problem, the unequal impact of the policies and procedures is. If one group of students are most impacted by a discipline policy, the deficiency may be in the policy, not the students.

Data seems to indicate that training is desperately needed to get end-users of disciplinary policies to stop weaponizing the policies against African-American students. Ironically, the policies created during the zero-tolerance era (designed to consequence students for bringing weapons) are instead used to assign disciplinary consequences to much less severe behaviors ("Zero Tolerance Policies Are Not as Effective as Thought," 2006). And those consequences are typically harsh; they are not instructive, therapeutic, or restorative for students or the campus community (Smith, Fisher, & Frey, 2015). With the advent of technology and funding streams for staffing to address safety, schools have become efficient at issuing out-of-school consequences to students who display so-called disobedient and disruptive behaviors. Back in the day, school districts processed paperwork for disciplinary infractions using carbon paper forms. They wrote behavior referrals by hand. Now, schools have databases and software programs that allow employees to issue out-of-school consequences for students with the click of a button. Automation reduces reflection. School staff members no longer have to reflect on situations as they did back when they were handwriting behavior referrals and documentation for out-of-school consequences. The process to put kids out of school has become strikingly efficient. Increased efficiency leads to more students needing to be seen by disciplinary staff members, so schools have had to hire more people to keep pace with the speed technology allows schools to generate behavior referrals. Technology has shortened the time it takes to put a student in the school-to-prison pipeline.

The umbrella of zero-tolerance policies, similar to how Jim Crow laws operated during the Reconstruction period of American history, makes it easy for schools and districts to function this way. Impatience or intolerance for therapeutic responses to students' poor behavior choices, a sentiment born out of the zero-tolerance era of school discipline, has not helped. It is significant to note that the American Federation of Teachers once supported zero-tolerance policies but reversed course. The Federation realized that zero-tolerance policies were wrong and negatively impacted students (Winter, 2020).

Sometimes Structural Barriers Aren't the Reason for Disproportionate Suspensions. A Principal Sometimes Must Respond to Unique Circumstances

Show me a school with high suspension and expulsion rates, and I'll usually be able to point out one of three (or so) things happening:

- ◆ One—there is a principal at the school bringing order to a place that an outgoing principal (or principals) allowed to devolve into disorder and 'off-the-hook' behaviors.
- ◆ Two—there is a principal at the school responding to an uptick in unacceptable behaviors. He or she is temporarily engaging in disproportionate suspension and expulsion to unearth and address the root cause of the increased undesirable actions. Admittedly, district officials must

monitor closely as this increased rate should not occur for an extended period. A rise in gang activity in the 'walk zone' of the school can be a common cause. Or it could occur when there is not enough support from school districts (or the juvenile justice system) when students released from prison are placed back on comprehensive school campuses.

◆ Three—there is a principal at the school who needs support. He or she is working to stop their staff from engaging in systematic, disproportionate suspension and expulsion of students of color at rates higher than similarly situated schools in the same (or similar) districts. There is little to no reason why schools in the same region with the same demographics should suspend and expel students at strikingly different rates. When this happens, there is a problem with leadership. And it's not necessarily a problem with leadership at the site level. The supervisors of principals are, at times, insurmountable barriers to schools' and school leaders' success. Sometimes, it is a school principal's supervisor who must be removed for a school and school leader to succeed.

◆ Three and a half—the principal and their supervisor are amenable to the disproportionate suspension and expulsion of students. This situation occurs when the issues from point three are in place, and the leaders are proud of the fact they suspend students of color.

When I inherited my school, I inherited a number-three type of situation. A quarter of my administrative team might have been bigots. Two of them openly shared in an office of African-American support staff members that I got promoted to principal solely because I was Black. A respected Caucasian licensed staff member openly told African-American support staff employees that my school's efforts to push and encourage African-American students to graduate was a waste of time. I even had a Caucasian superior threaten to serve me with a disciplinary document for changing failed practices and policies that resulted in my school only graduating 65% of its students. At that time, the Caucasian superior at the district level was a formidable barrier to progress.

Zero-tolerance was not my school's official disciplinary policy. However, the spirit of intolerance that fuels zero-tolerance policies underpinned how a significant number of teachers reacted to misbehavior in classrooms. I believe that's why my school had been suspending African-American students five times more frequently than any other group of students, though African-American students were only a third of the school's student population. This was a rate we were about to change.

Sudden Success Earned Us 'Haters'

Shortly after launching the Restorative Justice Tribunal, suspension rates decreased. We heard 434 cases in the first school year, only had to refer five cases back to administrators and achieved a 98.8% success rate. The next school year, we heard 174 restorative justice cases. We only had to refer three cases back to administrators, earning a 98.3% success rate. The school year after that, we heard 125 restorative justice cases and only had to refer five cases back to administration, earning a 95.9% success rate, and the year Covid-19 hit, Restorative Justice Facilitators heard 63 cases, and none of the offenders had to be referred back to administration. In total, the program's success rate was 98.9%. Relative risk ratio is how disproportionality is typically measured. If a group of students has a relative risk ratio over 2.0 for two consecutive years, they are considered disproportionately overrepresented in the data. My school's relative risk ratio for African-American students in the 2018–2019 school year, in one of the toughest schools in the district with one of the largest African-American populations, was 1.9.

The success of our restorative justice program and efforts to derail Jim Crow discipline earned us speaking engagements at conferences and got pursued by the press for interviews. The process had become so successful that I'd begun training school leaders statewide to start restorative justice programs in their schools. We'd begun hosting groups of educators at my school to train them in restorative practices.

However, sudden success made us a target. A so-called expert got into the ear of an influential leader in my district and convinced them that without Circles there was no restorative justice.

That's craziness.

That belief was the most idiotic, misinformed thing I had ever heard, especially given our results. Because I refused to use Circles as a primary medium to facilitate restorative practices, this leader undermined funding for our program. That influential leader played a part in slowing the flow of funds earmarked by our state legislature to add a counseling component to our Restorative Justice Tribunal program. The counseling would have allowed us to provide therapy to students and families for free, even to undocumented students, regardless of if the students or families had health insurance. The proposed funding would have been a dream come true as it would have put us in a position to help a lot of children and their families. The influential leader took a large sip of 'haterade' and dashed the dream. The obstructionism was absolute craziness. Put another way, there were haters in the game.

Aside from the haters, I can't deny we experienced some self-inflicted wounds that were totally my fault. There were a number of people on my staff who excelled at building relationships with students and could help their colleagues become better at maintaining order in their classes. There was, without question, enough teachers who could lead (or at minimum support) an effort to explore existing implicit biases. These staff members could engage their peers in a courageous conversation about the school's disproportionate suspensions and expulsions of African-American students. It didn't happen. I created this barrier, and in hindsight it was the wrong decision. Like previously mentioned, teachers' were upset over their teaching contract, so I didn't want to ask staff members to take on 'one more thing' or to facilitate 'one more conversation.'

In hindsight, I probably should have taken a gamble and asked staff for their help leading a schoolwide discussion about disproportionate suspensions and expulsions. I don't think we lost major ground in our implementation of restorative justice; however, because school policing was not going well in some schools around the country, I wish I would have asked my staff, including my amazing school police officers, to engage our school community in a conversation about disproportionality, including how school police can help slow the school-to-prison pipeline. If I had made this happen, more students who saw our school police as enemies instead of allies might have made different choices in their behavior, particularly when they were engaging in criminal behavior.

Important Relationship With School Police

Technology has allowed schools to issue behavior consequences to students faster than ever before, and that added efficiency has prompted some schools to increase the number of personnel in schools dedicated to maintaining order, including increasing the number of school police officers on campuses. I personally support schools being assigned an appropriate number of well-trained police officers.

This is an era where, for the sake of everyone's safety, one has to take preventative steps to ensure both students and adults are safe on school campuses. As a school leader, I want everyone in my school to feel safe to learn, work, and visit. However, problems emerge when schools or districts rely too much on police to maintain orderly learning environments. Put another way, the school-to-prison pipeline gets wider and shorter when schools outsource discipline enforcement to police officers. This is a slippery slope, and it should not happen.

Police officers are trained to de-escalate situations when people behave unlawfully. They do not receive extensive training in how to de-escalate classroom misbehavior. Police officers are not taught how to keep elementary school students sitting in their assigned seats or how to respond when the students flat out refuse to do so. Nor are police officers trained to dissuade secondary students from spreading rumors about peers who used to be their friends and who inexplicably become their archenemies because of a questionable social media post.

These normal school-based distractions are not crimes, and I do not believe these situations should be outsourced to school police officers. However, when students' defiance increases to highly disruptive levels, these situations sometimes get referred to police for their intervention and end up as arrests. When police presence increases on school campuses, arrests tend to increase. That is a fact. Most schools that have police officers on staff are schools that tend to have more students of color. This is also a fact. For this reason, it is often argued that the disproportionate rate of arrests of African-American students is circumstantial.

That argument falls apart under closer analysis. An overwhelming majority of school-related arrests that are referred to outside law enforcement—regardless of the racial demographics of schools—are arrests of African-American students. The figures reveal ongoing unbalanced rates of students entering the school-to-prison pipeline. However, I have to share something about my experience working with school police in my school and district. It appears to be very different from the experience of some of my peers in school administration. The police officers I work with make arrests. But they are never silly arrests, and I rarely see our police officers go 'hands-on' with students unless it is strikingly clear that they have no other choice in order to protect themselves or others.

Let me explain. Kids get arrested in my school for possession or distribution of controlled substances, possession of a firearm, or when they fight and the fight causes a substantial disruption to the normal functioning of the school. And when I say substantial, I am not talking about a scuffle that is easily regarded as a bother or a nuisance. I am referring to the chaos of multiple students engaging in multiple skirmishes. Staff members, up to and including the school police, may have to physically intervene to stop the fighting as we all hope that the cops don't have to use pepper spray to disperse the crowd or subdue combatants.

When I go around the country and talk about my experience with school police, I always acknowledge how I know my experience with school-based police officers may be unique. Unlike some school districts, the Clark County School District in Las Vegas, Nevada, has its very own police force. This force is the largest school police force in Nevada. Clark County School District Police don't function like officers in some other school districts. Clark County School District Police Officers carry guns, make arrests, and are trained to use lethal force, though they rarely ever need to do so.

Another thing that's unique about the Clark County School District Police Force is they are remarkably, exceptionally effective at community policing. Community policing is a cornerstone of the approach to improving relationships between communities and the police and reducing arrests. Community policing is a law enforcement philosophy that allows officers to remain in the same areas for extended periods to establish stronger relationship bonds with community members. This positions officers to be much more preventative in their approaches, rather than reactive to crime. When done well, the officers become members of the community and are not considered outsiders. Also, the officers develop an investment in the communities they serve.

For schools with officers, I believe community policing is a vital component of reducing suspensions and expulsions. This belief is particularly important now that more schools are outsourcing behavior management responsibilities to school-based police officers. Since I became the principal of my school, I've had five personnel combinations of a two-officer team assigned to my campus. For most of that time, one officer, Officer McNeil, was a fixture in the campus community—thus adhering to basic concepts of community policing.

Officer McNeil arrived at my school around the same time I arrived as principal. Neil, as we affectionately called him, was a standout dude. He would take food to hungry families, find coats and jackets for cold children, and pay students' fees and fines when their families couldn't afford to do so. Neil was someone moms and dads would call directly to stop conflicts before they started—particularly if the conflicts were gang-related. Here is the kicker. Often the families Neil engaged with were the families of students whom he detained (on suspicion of a crime) or arrested. Others he engaged with were released from jail, people who sought his help to navigate tough (and sometimes dangerous) social situations, or students who he established relationships with during the normal course of his job.

Neil was dialed in with, and close to, some of the most violent people in North Las Vegas. Together we used unofficial channels of communication and community partnerships to keep the campus safe. It was textbook community policing, all happening through the school. Officer McNeil's partners changed periodically, but every Clark County School District Police Officer I've worked with had a common skill—they all interacted with children expertly. Officer McNeil eventually transferred to a different position with more leadership responsibilities. Still, the officers that followed him all demonstrated the same skill. Their effective interactions are enhanced by community policing.

I'll never forget one morning when two young ladies got into a fight right before the bell rang to go to first period classes. Neil had moved on to his new role in the district when this fight happened, and my school had new school police officers assigned to our campus. It's hard to forget that morning or that fight because both girls were bigger than me. They were just about bigger than every one of us on the administrative team at that time. Because the young ladies would not stop hitting each other when officers, staff, and I physically intervened and used verbal commands, the officers dispersed pepper spray to subdue them.

Of course, I swallowed a mouthful of the pepper spray during the fray. And the pepper spray went all up in my nose like I was Little Seymour in the movie *Uptown Saturday Night* (youngsters, look up the movie). I also ripped the seam beneath the right-hand pant pocket of one of my favorite suits while restraining one of the young ladies who was fighting. I'm still pretty upset about that, and that's another reason I will remember that rumble.

What happened next illustrated the power of community policing and validated its use in my school. One officer was restraining one of the young ladies by her arm, and she was complying. As he walked her away from the scene, he yelled at her. But it was not like a police officer commanding a situation on the streets. Rather, he yelled like an angry (actually, a pissed off) father giving his child 'the business' in front of her friends. Though the officer was a young man, his face was unmistakably 'old school stern' as he yelled at her, "I told you not to do this! Didn't I tell you not to do this!"

That moment communicated two things to me as the 'principal teacher' of the school. Firstly, the officer had intervened before the fight to try to help the student avoid the conflict before it started, which I appreciated very much. Secondly, he was primarily upset because the student was 'hard-headed' and hadn't listened to his counsel. That's just one illustration. I could share many more.

It didn't matter if a student was a regular education student, special education student who was severely autistic, or special education student with severe emotional or behavioral disabilities. Every officer I have had the pleasure of working with demonstrated remarkable skill at communicating and influencing students' behavior without using force, regardless of the students' gender, race, or ability. I don't think I fully appreciated how unique my experience was with school police officers until I began doing research for this book and talking with teachers, leaders, and police officers across the country about their experiences in schools. In some schools, police officers are regarded as 'bullies in blue' and contribute to the criminalization of school-aged children. Frankly, some of the stories are heartbreaking.

Because of my experiences with well-trained school police officers, I cannot understand the need to zip-tie the hands of elementary school children, arrest them, and have their parents pick them up from a police station (Swisher, 2020). I will never understand a School Resource Officer seeing a need to twist a defiant elementary student's arms painfully behind his back and carry him into a classroom (Mosqueda, Balonon-Rosen, Natarajan, & Craven, 2017). If a student has not broken the law, there is little need for an officer to intervene when students display run-of-the-mill naughty behavior. I am convinced that if school districts are going to address disproportionality in suspension and expulsions, they must reconsider the training of school resource officers and police officers. The daily supervision, performance expectations, and professional standards, especially for school resource officers and campus security monitors, must be reviewed. They must also understand how their speech, actions, and use of authority affects others in the school community. Officers need to know how to repair any harms that occur when they (sometimes unknowingly) cause damage in the community while carrying out their duties.

There is such a critical need for restorative practices on school campuses. When schools and school districts can help students feel safe and secure through fair and effective disciplinary practices, students will feel more comfortable engaging academically.

References

Mosqueda, P., Balonon-Rosen, M., Natarajan, R., & Craven, M. (2017, November 14). *Ending excessive force in schools*. Retrieved from www.endzerotolerance.org/single-post/2017/11/14/Ending-Excessive-Force-in-Schools

Smith, D., Fisher, D., & Frey, N. (2015). *Chapter 1. Punitive or restorative: The choice is yours*. Retrieved from www.ascd.org/publications/books/116005/chapters/Punitive-or-Restorative@-The-Choice-Is-Yours.aspx

Swisher, S. (2020). *A 6-year-old had her hands zip-tied at school. Florida house passes on setting a minimum age for arresting kids*. Retrieved from www.sun-sentinel.com/news/politics/fl-ne-school-safety-bill-house-approval-20200304-ety42eskxncq3n7uchx3amysdu-story.html

Winter, C. (2020). *Amid evidence zero tolerance doesn't work, schools reverse themselves*. Retrieved from www.apmreports.org/episode/2016/08/25/reforming-school-discipline

Zero tolerance policies are not as effective as thought. (2006). [Press release]. Retrieved from www.apa.org/news/press/releases/2006/08/zero-tolerance

Further Reading

https://curry.virginia.edu/faculty-research/centers-labs-projects/research-labs/
    youth-violence-project/violence-schools-and-1
https://law.jrank.org/pages/1649/Police-Community-Policing-Origins-
    evolution-community-policing.html

5

A Pressure Cooker of Expectations

Safety Matters: Maslow Before Blooms

As discussed, I believe safety and order are prerequisites for students to learn and for teachers to educate effectively. I don't see how teaching and learning take place in classrooms that are 'off the hook' in terms of behavior. Orderly, organized instruction is a prerequisite for excellent academic outcomes. This is nothing new. This isn't a novel idea. This notion of safety and security being essential to learning is instinctive to parents, and it is the foundation of Maslow's Hierarchy of Needs. Given this, I see why some school personnel, who believe they cannot maintain order, outsource the maintenance of some school disciplinary functions to school police officers.

Some schools, without question, lack resources they need to keep students and employees safe on school campuses. Too often, there is a disconnect between how safe school staff feel and the degree to which their districts believe they are meeting their responsibility to provide tools, resources, and the training necessary to keep schools and the people in them safe.

It is common to hear school personnel say:

◆ We don't have adequate camera surveillance capabilities in our school.
◆ We don't have enough school resource officers (if they have any officers).
◆ We don't have enough school police officers (if they have any police officers).
◆ We have the authority to issue consequences to students who misbehave or who commit crimes.

I could go on. It is easy to understand how continually feeling overexposed to harm can be frustrating for a school community. That exasperation undermines teaching and learning. Added to this frustration is downward pressure on teachers and school leaders that all students in all schools must achieve. Schools must earn the correct 'grade,' get favorable 'star ratings,' get great scores on standardized tests, and get high percentages of students to graduate. I completely believe these outcomes are possible, even in the presence of a perpetual overexposure to feelings of potential danger or harm. With hard work, amazing staff, and (in my opinion) by God's grace, I've had the fortune of turning around three secondary schools where these feelings of overexposure to harm existed, so I know it's possible.

However, just because it's possible to succeed under these circumstances doesn't make it advisable, let alone right. I believe this pressure on school leaders and school staff is unhealthy. Heroically, the leaders and staff members in these schools persist and strive to achieve success under circumstances that many would deem improbable (if not impossible). And yet we wonder why the attrition rate in America's most challenging schools for all job classifications is so much higher than the attrition rates for job classifications in other schools.

Some school leaders approach these situations being mindful of balancing school achievement benchmarks and metrics without jettisoning hard-to-teach and hard-to-reach students out of school through suspensions and expulsions. However, when the achievement levels are not optimal and academic benchmarks and metrics are threatened; when resources and support are scarce, and the pressure for teachers and leaders to succeed is enormous, many begin to do whatever they must to relieve that pressure. Unfortunately, too many schools choose to remove any variables that act as stresses—up to and including students. Out-of-school consequences get used to deal with nuisance infractions, not true safety concerns or persistent threats to teaching and learning.

Restorative justice practices are a better solution for students who commit low-level behavior infraction—the infractions that are nuisances but not threats to learning or school safety. Restorative practices such as the Restorative Justice Tribunal help students understand how their behavior impacts the learning of others in the classroom and school community. It allows them to repair harms their behavior causes.

Safety From Unfair Labels and Biased Beliefs

The behavior management approach that a school adopts must minimize disruptions to instructional time and protect the sanctity of the learning community. It must also promote reflection by students and teachers that leads to relationship building and (when necessary) individual behavior change. Even if you remove the name 'Restorative Justice' from the behavior intervention you are about to learn, any approach should have these goals in mind. This will ensure a long-term positive impact on the school community.

School consumers, like the rest of the public, tend to gravitate toward what's new and shiny. Granted, there is a novelty to restorative practices. However, I don't think there is anything new about helping a person reflect on their behavior, identify dissonance in their beliefs and actions, and creating a space for them to reshape their beliefs in ways that minimizes/eliminates that discord. This is simply using principles of Cognitive Behavioral Therapy as the foundation of a schoolwide behavior management approach. These principles are not new, but they have been shaped to work in schools. This school-based intervention for students is designed to be (optimally) implemented over a short time by a school counselor, social worker, and/or school psychologist.

In my opinion, schools must free these professionals, especially school counselors and school social workers, from the myriad of non-counseling tasks they tend to be assigned, so they have time to provide more psychosocial and behavioral supports to students and staff. Increasing school counselors and social workers' reach and focus with students (especially) is essential if schools and districts are to increase their odds of success at reducing disproportionate suspension and expulsion through restorative (or any other) practices.

When done well, restorative justice can disrupt the gross overrepresentation of students of color that receive out-of-school disciplinary consequences. Some believe it is socioeconomic status, more than race, that accounts for the disproportionality that exists between the suspension and expulsion rates of African-American students and their peers. The data does not bear this out. Disproportionate racial representation in suspension and expulsion rates remains a reality even after one controls for the socioeconomic status of students (Hanson, 2011).

Some people rationalize away the racial differences in suspension and expulsion by claiming that African-American youth engage in more severe behaviors that warrant harsher discipline. The data doesn't bear this out either. In the aggregate, African-American youth do not receive more disciplinary referrals for more severe behavior in schools. Actually, African-American students disproportionately receive more discipline referrals for subjective and non-violent offenses, such as making too much noise in class or for being perceived as being disrespectful to their teachers.

In research of disproportionality in suspension and expulsions, researchers consistently find that African-American students are overrepresented in exclusionary discipline consequences. This is regardless of the way disproportionality was measured and defined by the researchers ("Black-White Achievement Gaps Go Hand in Hand With Discipline Disparities"). How schools label students is an essential cog in the machinery that churns students out into the school-to-prison pipeline. How something is defined influences how people think about it. Too often school communities label students subjected to out-of-school disciplinary consequences as troublemakers. This classification is increasingly problematic for students who receive multiple suspensions for subjective and non-violent offenses. It is difficult for them to break free of the 'troublemaker' label.

For African-American students, the label of troublemaker too often evolves to 'dangerous,' even in the absence of actual dangerous behavior. There's little, if anything, that's dangerous about a 'mouthy' child who refuses to sit in his or her assigned seat or who becomes defiant because they are slow to stop talking in class when directed. However, these students are the ones that tend to get labeled as 'dangerous' over time, not because they pose an actual physical threat to anyone but because they undermine adults' authority. It is notable that among students who are classified by school staffs as overly aggressive, African-American students receive more disciplinary consequences than any other group ("Racial Disproportionality in School Discipline: Implicit Bias is Heavily Implicated"). Interestingly enough, what causes variation in this trend is the racial background of teachers. Researchers found that once Black and White students were placed with same-race teachers, Black students' classroom behavior was rated more favorably by Black teachers than by White teachers (Lindsay & Hart, 2017). This makes me wonder how much the racial background of teachers and school leaders factors into schools suspension and expulsion rates. When educators lack cultural self-awareness and are not aware of implicit biases, negative perceptions of students of color increase.

So what is an implicit bias? Implicit biases are the mental processes that cause us to have negative feelings and attitudes about people based on characteristics such as race, ethnicity, age, and appearance. Implicit bias is often unconscious. We typically aren't aware of these negative biases we develop over our lifetimes. Lack of cultural self-awareness and implicit bias are contributing factors when we analyze unbalanced racial rates in school discipline. When school communities are unaware of implicit biases, stereotypes of Black students (particularly poor Black students) as unruly, disruptive, disrespectful, or dangerous can seep into the social fabric and programming of schools.

In an ideal world, teachers and school administrators would be immune to these unconscious negative attitudes and predispositions about race. Of course, they're not immune; school staff members are human, and they bring who they are into schools and classrooms. The disproportionate suspensions of these so-called 'dangerous' students too often lead to students' removal to alternative education settings, some of which are managed by the juvenile justice system. Restorative justice programming disrupts this trend by diverting students from the pathway to the juvenile justice system by short-circuiting suspensions for low-level behavioral offenses.

School counselors, school-based social workers, and school-based psychologists can play a critical role in schools' restorative justice programming. A well-run restorative justice program will provide students with strategies to identify behaviors and manage situations that lead to referrals to the administrators for low-level behavioral infractions. An effective restorative justice program also helps teachers form relationships with students. The Restorative Justice Tribunal helps teachers understand how their adult behaviors may cause students to react to them in ways that unnecessarily disrupt the classroom environment.

When done correctly, restorative practices upend the trends that lead to the overrepresentation of any group of students in exclusionary disciplinary practices.

Use Data to Relieve the Pressure—A Call for Intervention

My school's restorative justice program used disciplinary data as a thermometer to check the health and wellness of both the program and the overall campus disciplinary response structures. When disciplinary referrals or suspensions rates were trending in the wrong direction, I knew I needed to redirect the work of staff members. When the school-to-prison pipeline machinery is running at full steam and disproportionality is running amok, low-level disciplinary infraction data is most likely not being used to identify students needing intervention.

I liken using disciplinary data to check the health and wellness of disciplinary response structures to using a thermometer to see if a child is sick. If a child's temperature is at 99 or 100 degrees, I'm concerned. That's like if there is small spike in discipline data for a week or month or if a teacher writes an unusually high number of referrals in comparison to his or her peers. If there is a giant leap in suspension and expulsion data, then a school's response should be more urgent. That's like taking a child's temperature, and the thermometer reading reaches 103 degrees or higher. That data point can't be ignored. The child's health depends on urgent, decisive action.

Instead of using the discipline data to identify students (or teachers) in need of instructional or behavioral assistance, disciplinary data is too often used to target students for removal from school. When schools use discipline data to focus primarily on students' poor behavior choices rather than on the background for those choices, schools miss opportunities to help students be successful. Also, when schools focus on outcome behaviors rather than causes of the behavior, they are more likely to increase the number of 'truants and troublemakers.' Staff tend to target these students for removal from school. Exclusionary disciplinary practices result in a loss of instructional time, and loss of instructional time often correlates with an increase in problematic behavior. It is, indeed, a vicious cycle.

The difficulty of students labeled by schools as 'truants and troublemakers' becomes more acute when staff perceive these students' parents and guardians as powerless to prevent their child's removal from school. When this happens, school personnel tend to be more aggressive in their actions to jettison students from the school. The school-to-prison pipeline becomes even more efficient. Even though suspension is the widely used strategy in schools to modify and redirect students' behavior, suspensions tend to impact the same students significantly. Put another way, the same students tend to be suspended repeatedly, which suggests that suspension does not work as a deterrent to poor behavior choices.

This is why more therapeutic approaches are needed, such as the restorative justice approach proposed in this book. Also, this is why school counselors, social workers, and school psychologists must be given more opportunities to provide therapeutic interventions that reduce suspensions. At a minimum, their administrative tasks need to be simplified. Doing so allows them to spend more time providing essential services. Services include short-term counseling, analyzing discipline data, referring students to appropriate community resources, and supporting students' overall success. I believe all these professional responsibilities will mitigate suspension and expulsion of all students.

References

Black-White achievement gaps go hand in hand with discipline disparities. (2019, October 22). Retrieved from www.edweek.org/ew/articles/2019/10/16/black-white-achievement-gaps-go-hand.html

Hanson, J. E. (2011, September 24). *Jim Crow laws and racial segregation.* Retrieved from https://socialwelfare.library.vcu.edu/eras/civil-war-reconstruction/jim-crow-laws-andracial-segregation/

Lindsay, C., & Hart, C. (2017). Exposure to same race teachers and student disciplinary outcomes for Black students in North Carolina. *Education Evaluation and Policy Analysis, 39*(3), 25.

Racial disproportionality in school discipline: Implicit bias is heavily implicated (February 5). Retrieved from http://kirwaninstitute.osu.edu/racial-disproportionality-in-school-discipline-implicit-bias-is-heavily-implicated/

6

Jim Crow Discipline

Pressure to Keep Order in Classrooms

Tell me if this anecdote sounds familiar to you. In a classroom of diverse students, a teacher asserts their authority in a way that students perceive as unfair. A student assumes the role of an advocate for his or her peers. That student is then singled out to be removed for insubordination. The student is perceived by his or her teacher as a threat to their authority and classroom control. The last thing the teacher wants is to 'lose control' of their classroom.

Disproportionately, the students at the receiving end of disciplinary consequences in this scenario are African-American students. The threat *is* a perception, and the scenario is common. In fact, it is very common and characterizes the anxiety classroom teachers experience about losing control of their class to a student they perceive as unruly. That anxiety drives some teachers to wield suspension and expulsion as their weapon of choice to maintain control of their classrooms.

Due to the professional cost of having a classroom one's peers perceive as unruly, it is easy to understand why these anxieties exist. What teacher wants a class of students who disregard directions and classroom structures? That could make days on the job long and difficult. What teacher wants a conga line of supervisors in their class, observing them regularly because their students are off the hook and their classroom management is questionable?

Besides maintaining classroom order, teachers are expected to get all students to demonstrate academic growth and success. Getting all students to demonstrate academic growth is hard in classrooms that aren't orderly. The inability of a teacher to get students to focus on standards (or anything else in their class) greatly undermines academic outcomes for all students. Not only teachers but also school leaders are held accountable for orderliness in classrooms. The mere perception that a teacher's classroom environment is not conducive to teaching and learning prompts school leaders to feel pressure to 'get it together' and supervise these teachers more closely. All of this drives teachers' anxieties about maintaining order and control in their classes. It motivates them to use whatever tools they have at their disposal to keep students focused on standards and to sanction students whose behavior choices undermine their ability to teach.

Unfortunately, over 30 years of research has consistently shown that African-American students disproportionately experience the brunt of these sanctions. Often, teachers and schools establish a fixed perception of how a classroom should look, sound, and feel to them and other students. On its face, this makes sense. It is reasonable to expect a set of behavioral norms for members of a classroom community. These behavioral norms and the associated expectations are influenced by the personal experiences of teachers and school leaders. That makes sense too.

These behavioral norms are rooted in social standards that dictate how people expect students to behave. Social norms, in turn, are influenced by the cultural experiences of teachers and those who engineer the culture and climate of a school. When students threaten or don't adhere to the social (written or unwritten) norms of classrooms, the school community typically conspires (sometimes unconsciously) to compel compliance. Whenever students aren't perceived as fitting within these rules or social norms, they are often labeled as troublemakers. They then become prime targets for any tool at a school or teacher's disposal—such as suspension and expulsion—to compel adherence to behavioral expectations.

Unfortunately, the data bears out that African-American students find themselves disproportionately targeted because of the fear and anxiety of losing control that teachers experience. It is teachers' fear of losing control—rather than the actual threat of experiencing danger—that elevates benign misbehavior by African-American students into proverbial mountains that appear to merit out-of-school consequences as a remedy.

The pressure that school leaders feel to demonstrate quantifiable school success dramatically increases the likelihood of harsh reactions to students' misbehavior. Instead of responding proportionally to benign misbehavior from students of color, teachers and administrators are more likely to remove students who don't fit into the behavioral norms of the general student population. I believe there are frightening parallels between the ways classrooms, schools, and districts write and enforce discipline policies that supposedly maintain safety and order in schools for all children and Jim Crow policies that disenfranchised African-Americans at the turn of the 20th century. Modern-era Jim Crow discipline policies allow whimsical school personnel to terrorize disenfranchised families and their children. Suspension and expulsion become weapons to enforce compliance to modern-era school-based Jim Crow expectations and structures.

Restorative justice and restorative practices can short-circuit these policies. Restorative practices may need legislative champions to reverse the trend of disproportionate suspension and expulsions of African-American students in school districts, just as heroes came forth during the Jim Crow era of American history.

What Is Jim Crow?

Let me talk a little bit about Jim Crow and then make a connection to schools. If you are not a fan of history, please indulge me for a moment. Jim Crow was a name given to a system of state laws designed to ensure the disenfranchisement of African-American people in the early 19th and 20th centuries, the period of American history known as Reconstruction. The Black Codes, also known as the Black Laws, were the foundation upon which Jim Crow was built. Like Jim Crow, the Black Codes were state laws passed by Southern states at the end of the Civil War. These laws were designed to maintain a status quo of African-American peoples' servitude in the South after the Civil War.

The laws were designed to maintain a caste system that existed in the south. The laws prevented free Black people from owning land, engaging in business, or moving freely in public places. Black people could not bear arms, vote, or participate in high wage professions. Violations of the Black Codes were dealt with harshly by local authorities because of the broad 'vagrancy' laws embedded in the Black Codes. The vagrancy laws gave those in authority the power to arrest free Black people for minor infractions and commit them to involuntary labor. Put simply, Whites in authority could make up an infraction, call it vagrancy, and send free Black people to a life of bondage.

During the Black Codes and Jim Crow era, Black men were arrested for not having jobs or for having jobs that did not benefit White people. Jim Crow was nothing more than an extension of the Black Codes and a way to nullify the rights that Constitutional Amendments 13 and 14 extended to Black people. Jim Crow institutionalized 'separate but equal' as public policy. It entrenched segregated services: public transportation, public facilities, public health, and public education. However, as we now know, separate was never equal during the Jim Crow period of American history. Public amenities designated for use by people of color were grossly inadequate when compared to those designated for White people. Sometimes no separate facilities even existed for Black people to use.

With public schools, the 'separate but equal' resources allocated for students of color were horrifically inadequate when compared to schools for White children. Jim Crow schools only taught Black students Jim Crow skills (Irons, 2014). Jim Crow schools prepared Black students to be agricultural laborers and domestic servants to White people. From Delaware to Texas, schools in Jim Crow states spent three times as much money to educate White students than they did to educate African-American students (Irons, 2014). In the deep South, the funding inequities were even more dramatic. In Alabama, school boards spent five times more on the education of White students than they did on African-American students. In South Carolina, schools spent ten times more (Irons, 2014). This resulted in schools that served Black children perpetually having inadequate learning materials and facilities that seemed to remain in perpetual disarray.

The funding inadequacies to educate Black children in the Jim Crow South affected not only school facilities but also affected the experience of African-American teachers. Besides having to teach in substandard schools with inferior learning materials, African-American teachers were grossly underpaid. African-American teachers only made 60% of the salary of White teachers (Irons, 2014). While African-American teachers may have been paid poorly, they were not necessarily poorly trained. However, the salary of African-American teachers did little to attract the best and brightest teachers to schools for Black children in the Jim Crow South. In 1954, state-sponsored segregation was ruled unconstitutional by the United States Supreme Court. It took another ten years (and additional supreme court rulings) to compel states to stop enforcing Jim Crow policies.

I believe that while Jim Crow laws have been deemed unconstitutional and African-American students enjoy the right to a free and appropriate public education, the vestiges of Jim Crow survive and manifest (among other places) in the disciplinary policies that govern public schools.

Jim Crow and Control of Black People

Remember, Jim Crow was ultimately a system of control. Like disciplinary strictures in a school, the point of Jim Crow was to sustain order and social norms. Jim Crow compelled the behavior of Black people in ways that were predictable and financially beneficial to White people. The vagrancy laws and the widely known consequences for violating the vagrancy laws all but guaranteed Black people's behavioral compliance.

A Black man could not offer to shake a White man's hand because it implied the African-American person believed they were equal to White people, which was unacceptable in the Jim Crow South. Blacks and Whites couldn't eat together. Black people could not hold hands with each other or show public affection toward one another. If a White person commanded a Black person to do something, that Black person could not challenge the White person's demands without the threat of quick and swift violence. Police had the authority to arrest Black people on White citizens' suspicions that a Black person was about to do something illegal or out of compliance with vagrancy laws. Any arrest for a vagrancy violation all but guaranteed that the Black person would be detained and fined.

Somewhat like today's problems with the bail bonds system, the fines given to Black people all but guaranteed they would end up in prison or labor camps. When Black people could not pay the fines, the prison system sentenced Black people to serve in chain gangs. Convicts were leased out to plantation owners and corporations as a means of cheap labor. Of course, this was all in the guise of being a means for Black people to pay off their fines.

The treatment of prisoners in chain gangs was widely known, and the reputation of violence toward Blacks in chain gangs served to compel the behavior of Black people. Prisoners serving in chain gangs were whipped and beaten to ensure they remain productive to whoever leased them, just like how slaves were beaten on plantations. Blacks were beaten and sometimes killed if they tried to escape the chain gang. Black people's fear of these consequences functioned as another means of controlling their behavior. This institutionalized the social norms White people in power desired of Black people in the Jim Crow South. It didn't matter that Black people's actions were within their constitutional rights. Jim Crow's public policy goal was to keep African-Americans at the bottom of a caste system. For a Black person to resist was the same as having a death wish. Even after slavery had been ruled as unconstitutional, Jim Crow allowed states to enact harsh consequences for Black people opposing Jim Crow.

Jim Crow Remnants in Modern-Day Disciplinary Systems

I believe the vestiges of Jim Crow public policy live on in public school disciplinary policies. Jim Crow discipline exists. States still enact laws that give schools the right to exact swift, harsh, and disproportionate punishments. The unfair impact of modern-day discipline policy leads me to believe that modern-day Black Codes exist. Public schools do not send African-American students from the schoolhouse into chain gang bondage. But schools do send disproportionate numbers of African-American students to schools run by the juvenile justice system. The 'Kids for Cash' scandal broke in 2009; Judge Mark A. Ciavarella sentenced approximately 3,000 children to detention centers for minor offenses, barring them from a fair high school journey ("Pennsylvania Judge Gets 28 Years in 'Kids for Cash' Case," 2015). And for students who do not land in prison schools, there's still a disproportionate number of African-American students whose disciplinary outcomes involve them in the juvenile justice system in some form.

States have given school districts the authority to use out-of-school disciplinary consequences (or the threat of) to beat students into submission to (sometimes) overzealous behavioral expectations. There are too many instances of the Black Codes' vagrancy laws remixed for a modern age. Suspensions and expulsions (or the threat thereof) are modern-day whips and hangmen nooses. In 2013, Kyle Thompson was jailed, then placed under house arrest and barred from school for six months after trying to retrieve his note that a teacher had confiscated (Roelofs, 2014). A 2015 lawsuit revealed that a school sheriff cuffed an eight-year-old and a nine-year-old student (one Latino, one African-American) and left them that way for at least 15 minutes. Their hands were too small for the cuffs, so they were shackled around the bicep. Their crime? The children were restrained for behaviors resulting from their ADHD ("Lawsuit filed after Kentucky deputy handcuffs 2 children," 2015).

In 2015, a 15-year-old girl was flipped to the floor and dragged from the classroom for failing to surrender her phone to a staff member (Faussett & Southall, 2015). The two students who filmed the incident and objected to the conduct were criminally charged for 'disturbing schools' while the officer was never charged. The 'disturbing schools' (zero-tolerance) law can result in criminal charges for actions that would only be considered vaguely annoying if done by adults. Such actions include using a phone in class, making 'fart' noises, spraying perfume, or for being 'obnoxious.' Having a criminal record 'which would normally be reserved for serious theft and assault-type actions' can bar children from voting, holding licenses, and future employment before they've even graduated, assuming they even get the chance to graduate. Black students are four times more likely to be charged under this law.

The underlying effect of Jim Crow lynchings during the Reconstruction period of American history was to control through fear. The victim served as a warning to others not to 'overstep.' These terrible actions rose from a belief that one race was 'lesser' than another—less human and more animal, requiring excessive force to subdue. This parallel between historical lynching and modern-day issues is what Dr. Karlos K. Hill refers to as the 'painful symmetry' of being subjected to excessive brutality (Hill, 2016). Dr Hill writes in relation to police killings of Black people, but the principle is the same for school discipline. An underpinning belief based on perceptions of race results in excessive responses for minor actions.

The American Civil Liberties Union (ACLU) notes 141 public complaints of excessive use of police force in schools between 2014 and 2016 (Mann et al., 2019). According to their 'Cops and No Counselors' study, Black students are arrested in schools between three and eight times more than their White peers. Nobody argues that it is in the interest of the public to ensure school classrooms are orderly places conducive for learning for all students. However, all truly means all—up to and including the population of students whose benign disciplinary infractions get them unnecessarily placed on a pathway to out-of-school consequences. The disparity of out-of-school consequences for African-American students stands out, compared to their Caucasian peers. One could argue that the public policy goal of orderly classrooms—that facilitate a free and appropriate public education for all students—is not intended to ensure free and appropriate public education for all African-American students.

It is hard for one to argue that a genuine interest in the educational success of all students exists when evidence shows one group of students clearly experience different disciplinary consequences. A free and appropriate public education does not exist for any group of students removed from it. Sometimes students are removed by forcibly dragging them from classrooms and away from the teachers who are supposed to help them achieve education standards. Jim Crow-style discipline has taken root in classes throughout the country. Schools need sensible discipline policies and practices with a robust therapeutic complement. Students and staff will then be enabled to create classroom climates conducive for all students to learn. One example of such is the Restorative Justice Tribunal approach this book suggests.

Disciplinary Structures as Jim Crow Systems

Jim Crow was anchored in the belief that White people were superior to African-American people in intelligence, morality, and civilized behavior. The sanctioned discrimination of Jim Crow occurred because African-American people, the targets of the discriminatory action, were regarded as fundamentally unlike their oppressors. When targets of mistreatment are regarded as less than human (as African-Americans were considered during legalized slavery), it is easier for both active oppressors and passive oppressors to rationalize and accept the abuse. They are deemed unworthy of the same treatment as their oppressors. Psychologically, it is much more acceptable for oppressors to submit another group of people to awful, stifling, unfair, and unjust treatment if it is done in the name of safety, decency, or in the name of God. This happened during Jim Crow.

In modern-day Jim Crow school discipline structures, awful, stifling, unfair, and unjust disciplinary practices operate in the name of learning, order, and safety. Most behavioral expectations in schools and classrooms appear reasonable on the surface. It is reasonable to expect students to mind the volume of their voices in classes when learning is taking place. It is reasonable to expect students to adhere to a classroom system for leaving their seats or for leaving the classroom. It is reasonable for a teacher to expect students to adhere to their requests and classroom directives. Teachers and schools establish behavior expectations in the name of learning, order, and safety, and there is absolutely nothing wrong or evil about that.

It is when classroom guidelines cease to increase the probability of learning for all students and morph into structures that exist solely to control others that behavioral expectations encounter a slippery slope. It is when enforcement of classroom rules gets divorced from learning goals that things become problematic. The goal of socializing students should never supersede the purpose of teaching. It is without question that safety, security, and order are prerequisites for classroom learning. However, when actions in the name of these values create a caste system for groups of students, it is in the public interest (let alone ethical) to do things differently.

This is why restorative practices matter. Schools have an ethical duty to ensure all students have equal opportunities to be academically successful. Restorative practices create a pathway to short-circuit educational caste systems that exist in some schools—existing in the name of safety, security, and order.

Unwavering, Suffocating Control

To dissolve disciplinary and academic caste systems that exist in schools, school personnel have to behave differently and reassess their beliefs about the learning of diverse students.

How people behave is anchored in what they believe and how they see the world. All people have preferences, biases, and affinities. That's normal. However, schools cannot and should not normalize a belief that a group of students can't or won't learn and are predisposed to engage in problematic behavior. This belief leads to the mess on our hands that we have right now—disproportionate suspensions and expulsions of students.

When this normalization of negative perceptions about a group occurs, schools' interest in controlling students typically increases. The ultimate purpose of educating students and providing all students with a free and appropriate public education cannot be eclipsed. When students, especially African-American students, resist control, their resistance tends to feed any unflattering biases that staff members may hold. This is the cycle that keeps the Jim Crow disciplinary caste systems in place. Often this tension between resistance and control anchors conversations about levels of respect between teachers and diverse students. It is not uncommon for school personnel to believe that students should 'respect' them solely because they are teachers.

Frankly, the belief that students should respect their teachers is aligned with my Southern sensibilities. I don't think it is unreasonable for young people to pay appropriate respect to their elders, particularly their teachers. However, mutual respect must exist between teachers and their students. School personnel's words and actions must demonstrate mutual respect as well as genuine care and concern for the well-being and education of all students. Absent mutual respect, it's inevitable for the ground to become fertile for the resistance from students that triggers aggressive systems of behavioral control. One could argue that classroom teachers need respect (and compliance) from students because it allows teachers to provide all students with an appropriate education. Again, I believe it is reasonable for teachers to demand a foundational level of respect and compliance from students. That said, learning environments reflecting an attitude of "Respect me, and please do what I ask you to do" is many worlds apart from learning environments that demonstrate "Respect me. Do what I tell you to do because I'm in charge and I said so."

Those are two vastly different sentiments that create two very different learning environments. Sometimes, the 'respect' school personnel demand of students isn't 'respect' at all. It is totalitarianism that dares anyone to challenge the power wielder. In these environments, students are expected to blindly accept the behavior expectations of adults. Even when expectations are blazingly unfair, students are expected to toe the line. A need to exert unwavering, suffocating control over others is similar to the attitudes and beliefs that sustained Jim Crow. Active and passive advocates of Jim Crow used 'the need to control' in the name of overall safety, order, and economic stability as key justifications for the inhumane treatment of freed slaves, the targets of Jim Crow policy.

Maintaining control over students in the name of order and campus safety remains a central justification in modern school disciplinary systems. This explanation is touted even when a by-product of the disciplinary policy is disparate academic outcomes and unbalanced suspension and expulsion rates among groups of students. The widespread impact of school suspension and expulsion policies have ravaged the achievement outcomes of students of color. Inexcusable percentages of African-American students have been barred from their right to a free and appropriate public education.

What's worse is though state and school officials recognize the disparate outcomes these discipline policies cause, the policies and practices continue. And sometimes these policies function chillingly similar to Jim Crow laws. Similarities include the placement of scores of African-American students in modern-day prison camps where parties benefit not through convict leasing as they did during Jim Crow but through legislative actions that award private prisons grants and contracts.

Beneficiaries of Jim Crow empowered their agents to incarcerate Black people for violating unfair social expectations disguised as vagrancy laws. Similarly, some discipline policies and practices in schools unnecessarily trap African-American students in the juvenile justice system. And sometimes schools unwittingly—and unfortunately sometimes intentionally— mobilize disciplinary lynch mobs that accelerate students' entry into the juvenile justice system. Without substantial revision to these practices and policies, we are all conspiring to bloat the industrial prison complex. We are all unwitting coconspirators in educational lynch mobbery.

What Is a Lynch Mob?

Some may think the term 'lynch mob' is too strong of a term to describe school personnel subjugating African-American students to suspensions and expulsions. I disagree. I suspect the families and students being disproportionately suspended, expelled, and cited by law enforcement officers for sometimes questionable charges may also disagree. Let me take a moment to discuss lynching and lynch mobs. I'll also make a few historical connections between the enforcement of Jim Crow behavioral expectations for African-American people and the sometimes overzealous enforcement of school disciplinary expectations.

Lynching was a horrific behavior modification tool that existed during Jim Crow. Law enforcement, in partnership with White citizens, used lynching to control Black people's behavior after slaves were freed in the pre-war South. Here is what typically happened during a lynching. First, a White person would accuse a Black person of breaking the law. The charges levied against the Black person were virtually always fake. Law enforcement officers would then arrest the Black person for their alleged crime. Instead of a legitimate judicial proceeding occurring, a group of White men (a lynch mob) would conspire with the law enforcement officer and take the Black person away.

After seizing the Black person, the lynch mob of White men would beat and torture the accused Black person and hang them by the neck with a rope from a tree. They would then set the Black person on fire in a public forum for all to see. Whole families would travel to see the lynching and often bring their small children along. After the lynched Black person was dead and their body was burned, White spectators would then dismember the burned Black person's body or cut away sections of the body. Lynch mob participants would distribute parts from the burned body as souvenirs from the lynching (Young, 2005).

Absolutely awful.

A rash of lynchings took place in the United States between 1882 and 1930, particularly in the South, and this lynch-mob justice was used to maintain the social order of a racist caste system. Lynch mobs would 'ride on' African-Americans in the South whenever African-American people attempted to assert themselves in ways misaligned with being the lowest members of the caste system that existed at that time. Behaviors that threatened the order of the racial caste system triggered lynchings. Lynching was a primary tool White Southerners used to suppress African-American voting and voter registration between 1892 and 1930. Newly freed slaves were lynched if they attempted to assume trades or get jobs upper-caste Whites felt were reserved for White people. If a White person felt a Black man simply looked at a White woman, The Black man was at risk of being lynched, regardless of if the accusation was true or not.

Let's make an even more direct connection between lynching, lynch mobs, and school-based discipline. Like race, caste systems are social constructs that maintain social order. Schools and classrooms, like society, have a social order with defined social expectations and norms. Former slave owners in the Southern states dictated the social hierarchy after Reconstruction, and the goal of the caste system they oversaw was to maintain the economic benefits of slavery. To do this, Southern states had to create policy and enforce laws that protected their economic interests and maintained the social caste system they desired. Legislative leaders in Southern states did what other dominant members of any other oppressive caste system have historically done to maintain a dominant position. They instituted policies and passed laws that allowed them to terrorize and intimidate lower-caste group members, so they complied with the dominant group's interests.

What school districts around the country (I believe overwhelmingly, unwittingly) have done with discipline policy is what legislators in Southern states did in their institution of the Black Codes and Jim Crow. Both institutions created policies and laws that formed conditions that make it extraordinarily difficult for African-American people to succeed. I believe most policy makers see the impacts of an appalling educational caste system that disenfranchises African-American students or, to some degree, makes it difficult for too many African-American students to get a free and appropriate public education. But despite knowing this, these influential people turn a blind eye. People in the Jim Crow South did too. There does not appear to be enough political will to address Jim Crow disciplinary practices. There does not appear to be enough discomfort with the current reality in schools to stop lynch mob behaviors from occurring.

When looking at the data, I don't know how one can say that lynch mobs don't exist in schools when African-American students are referred for suspension or expulsion more than five times more frequently than their peers; when African-American students are dragged out of classrooms; when elementary school students are handcuffed, arrested, and taken to police stations; and when schools ask for funding for the essential tools to keep campuses safe and legislative leaders can't (or don't) allocate the funds.

This modern-day lynch mob behavior suggested by the disparate suspension and expulsion rates for African-American students does not mortally wound students. But the behavior has a chilling effect that deeply affects African-American students academically and psychosocially. The impacts of this lynch mob behavior manifest in the low percentages of African-American students who are enrolled by schools in Advanced Placement classes or upper-level math classes. The lifelong effects of academic hamstringing show as achievement gaps in standardized test scores. Out of the top scorers on the math SAT in 2016, just 2% were African-American students, compared to 33% who were Whites (Reeves & Halikias, 2017). This gap has existed for years. However, psychometricians who help develop the exams refuse to acknowledge that something may be wrong with the tests. Despite the literature that points to racial bias in the tests, no significant changes have been made to them (Elsesser, 2019). This suggests that standardized test companies believe their tests have little to do with the huge disparity in scores between White students and African-American students. By default, this stance suggests test makers—and the school districts who use these tests—believe deficiency lies primarily in African-American students, and there is nothing wrong with the tests.

In my opinion, that's craziness.

So-called elite schools where students rarely receive out-of-school consequences are not immune from lynch mob behavior. Lynch mobbers in these schools use psychological warfare to terrorize African-American students. African-American students at these elite schools have reported that they have been unfairly graded, treated poorly by teachers, and allowed to be treated poorly by their peers. One such example is the case of racial discrimination discovered at Boston Latin School in 2016 (Wagner, 2016). The situation came to light when several brave students spoke out publicly about the racial tension African-American students at the school experienced. A subsequent federal investigation unearthed a pattern of race-based harassment at the school. The investigation found the school had not satisfactorily addressed repeated allegations of racial slurs, including a verbal threat by a student to lynch one of his female peers.

The students at Boston Latin are not alone in their experience with school-based racial discrimination. Throughout the country African-American students have told school leaders they feel they have been discriminated against or flat out terrorized by school staff. This lynch mob behavior occurs in some of the most competitive, exclusive secondary schools in the country, yet these cases are rarely investigated thoroughly. One rarely hears of significant changes occurring as a result of these students' reports. Therefore, the lynch mob behaviors and resulting student complaints continue. Too often, school district and legislative leaders behave like law enforcement officials did during Jim Crow—when officials conspired with lynch mobs to come and take falsely accused African-American people during the night to meet unconscionable abuse and torture. Except, in modern-day educational lynch mobbing, the abusers and torturers don't wait until the night; they feel free to do their deeds during the light of day, in plain sight for everyone to see.

References

Elsesser, K. (2019, December 11). *Lawsuit claims SAT and ACT are biased—here's what research says*. Retrieved from www.forbes.com/sites/kimelsesser/2019/12/11/lawsuit-claims-sat-and-act-are-biased-heres-what-research-says/?sh=36d6c4a3c429

Faussett, R., & Southall, A. (2015). *Video shows officer flipping student in South Carolina, prompting inquiry.* Retrieved from www.nytimes.com/2015/10/27/us/officers-classroom-fight-with-student-is-caught-on-video.html

Hill, K. (2016, March 3). *Are police shootings really like lynchings?* Retrieved from https://historynewsnetwork.org/article/162172

Irons, P. (2014). *Jim Crow's schools*. Retrieved from www.aft.org/periodical/american-educator/summer-2004/jim-crows-schools

Lawsuit filed after Kentucky deputy handcuffs 2 children. (2015). Retrieved from https://abc7news.com/kentucky-sheriff-handcuffs-two-children-with-disabilities-handcuffed-by-lawsuit-filed-for-handcuffing-keston-county-sheriffs-office/902369/

Mann, A., Whitaker, A., Torres-Gullien, S., Morton, M., Jordan, H., Coyle, S., & Sun, W.-L. (2019). *Cops & no counselors: How the lack of school mental health staff is harming students*. A report and blog post on high ratios of students to school psychologists for the American Civil Liberties Union (ACLU). Retrieved from https://www.aclu.org/report/cops-and-no-counselors

Pennsylvania judge gets 28 years in 'kids for cash' case. (2015, November 21). Retrieved from www.foxnews.com/us/pennsylvania-judge-gets-28-years-in-kids-for-cash-case

Reeves, R., & Halikias, D. (2017). *Race gaps in SAT scores highlight inequality and hinder upward mobility*. Brookings.

Roelofs, T. (2014, January 6). *A tussle over a note in class, then handcuffs*. Retrieved from www.bridgemi.com/talent-education/tussle-over-note-class-then-handcuffs

Wagner, M. (2016, April 8). *Headmaster of Boston Latin, nation's oldest public school, steps down amid allegations of campus racism*. Retrieved from www.nydailynews.com/news/national/headmaster-boston-latin-school-steps-race-scandal-article-1.2683666

Young, H. (2005). The black body as souvenir in American lynching. *Theatre Journal, 57*(4) 639–657.

For Further Reading

https://socialwelfare.library.vcu.edu/eras/civil-war-reconstruction/jim-crow-laws-andracial-segregation/

www.ferris.edu/jimcrow/what.htm

https://economics.yale.edu/sites/default/files/bad_men_good_roads_economics_of_chain_gang_v3_september_2020_ada-ns.pdf

https://cvltnation.com/lynchings-usa-fun-whole-family/

https://listverse.com/2016/04/13/10-gut-wrenching-stories-of-women-who-were-lynched/

www.theguardian.com/us-news/2018/apr/26/lynchings-memorial-us-south-montgomery-alabama

https://ahousedividedapd.com/2019/10/28/the-history-of-lynching-and-african-american-voting-rights/

7

Oversight, Academic Press, and Cultural Competence Derail Jim Crow Discipline

Suspension Can Turn Students' Lives Upside Down

Jamie was a tall, handsome African-American male student in the class of Ms. Dasalan, a Filipino math teacher. The cultural difference between Jamie and Ms. Dasalan should not have been a barrier to Jaime's success as Cheyenne had several Filipino teachers whose students were thriving. Unfortunately, this was not the case for Jaime and many of Ms. Dasalan's students.

Jamie was having a particularly difficult day with Ms. Dasalan. Jaime had difficulty mastering an algebraic concept in class, and he asked Ms. Dasalan for help. Ms. Dasalan knelt beside Jaime's desk and explained the steps to solve the problem again, but Jaime still didn't understand. According to Jaime, Ms. Dasalan stood up frustrated said the 'N-word' three times under her breath, referring to him and his peers in the class, and walked away from his desk. Jaime reacted, "I ain't nobody's [N-Word]!" and he walked out of the class.

Jaime was sent home on what many school districts call a Required Parent Conference (RPC). When a student is issued an RPC, a student is basically suspended until a school administrator has a scheduled conference with a student's family. The school has the authority to schedule that conference within two school days after a behavioral incident. This gives schools time to investigate incidents and make fair, appropriate decisions. I was determined to find the truth and either (1) remove the RPC from Jaime's record and investigate Ms. Dasalan for unprofessional conduct or (2) give Jaime consequences for walking out of class unauthorized. I just needed time to figure out what happened between Jaime and Ms. Dasalan.

The Deans' of Students investigated. They collected witness statements from thirteen students in Ms. Dasalan's class who were close to Jaime and Ms. Dasalan when the beef went down. Four witnesses, including Jaime, said Ms. Dasalan called Jaime and kids in class the N-word. Eight witnesses said they didn't hear Ms. Dasalan call Jaime the N-word, and one student said they didn't want to get involved. Ultimately, the investigation was inconclusive, and I could not substantiate Jaime's claims. Because the issue was so sensitive, dealing with racism and teacher discipline, I made the final decision. I brought Jaime back to school the day after we collected all the witness statements, giving him 'time served.'

Jaime was suspended out of school for one day, but that one-day suspension had a tremendous impact on Jaime as a person and on Jaime's relationship with his family. Jaime's sense of justice was shattered. Jaime was adamant that Ms. Dasalan called him the N-word, though we could not find evidence to support his claim. His family, for all intents and purposes, 'sided' with the school, and he saw that as his mom and dad betraying him. Throughout this entire situation, Jaime never wavered from his story. Ms. Dasalan had 'violated,' and he couldn't let that go, especially since he felt he had been punished when he was actually a victim. Jaime felt his family's unwillingness to fight for him to avoid suspension was unforgivable. Jaime stopped sharing his thoughts, feelings, and ideas about things happening in his life with his mom and dad. That suspension changed that family. Like the final note in a sad song, in his Post Conference with Ms. Green, Jaime asked, "Ms. Green, is this what discrimination feels like?"

Jim Crow Disciplinary Lynch Mob Terror

Unfortunately, Jaime's story is not unique. African-American students like Jaime are suspended far too often. I want to think the data is trending in the right direction, but that doesn't appear to be the case. In Portland Public Schools, Black students accounted for 46% of all major discipline incidents in middle schools. Their White peers only accounted for 5.2% (Jensen, 2020). In Massachusetts, Black girls are four times more likely to face school discipline than White girls (Solis, 2020). The Maryland State Board of Education recently verified that suspension and arrest rates are highest for Maryland's Black students, including unlawful suspensions for insubordination (Shwe, 2020). In Gwinnett County Public Schools, Georgia's largest school district, Black and Hispanic students comprise 64% of the student population but 85% of the out-of-school suspensions and expulsions (Center, 2020).

Implicit Bias and Discipline Policies

Throughout this book, I've pointed out connections between out-of-school consequences and academic achievement because I believe the two are connected. I don't believe that state legislators, district administrators, school leaders, or teachers (like Ms. Dasalan) set out to make decisions that harm students. I do think people sometimes unwittingly behave in ways that hurt children. I truly believe some staff are not conscious of the variables or biases they have that influence their decision-making and expectations.

This is the impact of implicit bias. Implicit bias is often based on prejudice or stereotypes. These prejudices cause people to make automatic judgments of a group's members. Lack of cultural self-awareness and implicit bias are contributing factors when we analyze unbalanced racial outcomes in school discipline data.

People act on stereotypical judgments or negative feelings from implicit biases without fully intending to do so. The converse is also true: implicit biases will delay or stop a person from acting, even if they know it is best to act.

Implicit bias has serious implications for disciplining students in schools. Implicit bias tends to affirm existing racial stereotypes and caricatures of Black youths. Unchecked implicit bias can have a cataclysmic effect on disciplinary outcomes for African-American students, particularly Black boys. This implicit bias phenomenon gets negatively compounded by sweeping, flawed generalizations of African-American males as irresponsible, dishonest, and dangerous.

Teachers who aren't unaware of their implicit biases fall prey to negative caricatures when they encounter African-American young men outside of their cultural experience. This phenomenon is nothing new. In a study that investigated teachers' perceptions of African-American students based on first impressions, researchers found that teachers perceived Black students who displayed a 'Black walking style' as lower in academic achievement, more aggressive, and in need of special education services (Rudd, 2014). Teachers also perceived these Black students as unruly, disruptive, disrespectful, and as students whose families did not value education.

While 'culturally competent' educators may find these ideas ridiculous, the fact remains that these perceptions of African-American students exist and are more widespread than folks realize. These caricatures of students of color, at times, undermine school employees' compassion for students that they perceive as different from themselves. This deficit of empathy is part of what makes lawmakers, policy influencers, and the public believe students of color being disciplined are 'getting what they deserve,' despite obvious disproportionality. Implicit biases take a lifetime to develop, and so become deeply entrenched (Staats, 2016). They influence who and what people care about and which groups people feel are worthy of care. It is easy for people to ignore implicit biases that contribute to developing this unconscious hierarchy of care.

As stated earlier, teachers and school administrators usually choose harsher punishments for African-American students than they do for White students, even for non-violent offenses. I believe this happens more frequently when school personnel are unaware of how implicit biases can influence decision-making. Awareness of implicit biases is something that must be strongly considered as an add-on to any restorative justice solution a school adopts to reduce suspension and expulsion of students. Challenging staff members' buried biases is an essential step to ensure fair opportunities for all students.

In the case of Jaime and Ms. Dasalan, the witness statements did not undeniably support Jaime's claim that Ms. Dasalan called him the N-word. However, I absolutely believe implicit racial bias played a role in Ms. Dasalan's expectations of Jaime and the academic and behavioral expectations she had of her class.

Implicit Bias and Academic Achievement

There is statistically significant evidence that teachers hold low expectations (either implicitly or explicitly) for African-American and Latino children compared to White children. Researchers found that as a result of teachers' implicit biases, African-American children are more likely than White children to confirm teachers' underestimation of their abilities. African-American students are also less likely to benefit from teachers' overestimation of ability (Copur-Gencturk, Cimpian, Lubienski, & Thacker, 2020).

Challenging the authority of a White person in the Jim Crow South could cost an African-American person his or her life. To draw a parallel, challenging the authority of modern-era teachers can cost an African-American student his or her future. Students pay a high cost when they lose instructional time due to removal from class for disciplinary purposes. Data from the administration of the 2017 National Assessment of Educational Progress (NAEP) validates this point. Researchers found that students with poor attendance in the month preceding NAEP assessments scored significantly lower than their peers who were in class (de Brey et al., 2019). It's hard to learn class content when you're not in class.

Researchers that studied the NAEP data also found that school-sanctioned absences negatively impacted students who weren't suspended. When teachers use instructional time to

address the gaps in learning for suspended students after returning from an out-of-school consequence, it appears to hurt everyone (Adams, 2015). Students returning from suspension
sometimes exhibited misbehavior. They struggled to understand
the class content they missed. When teachers have to stop teaching to manage this misbehavior, the rest of the class loses learning
time.

It is critically important that schools implement behavioral
interventions that help students navigate situations that put
them at risk of getting out-of-school behavioral consequences.
The Restorative Justice Tribunal does just that. In the absence of
diversion programs and structures to keep students in school
and clear from paths to out-of-school consequences, schools can
use suspension and the threat of suspensions to terrorize children
systemically.

A Need for Office of Civil Rights Oversight

I believe the reason why educational lynch mobbery hasn't run
completely amok is because the Civil Rights Division of the
United States Department of Justice during President Obama's
administration took action to prevent that. The Department's
intervention into disproportionality of suspensions and expulsions spawned a nationwide dialogue about school discipline
policies and how they impacted African-American students.

Mr. Eric Holder was the United States Attorney General
during President Obama's administration. Holder publicly
committed to dismantling the school-to-prison pipeline per-
petuated by disproportionate suspensions and expulsions.
Attorney General Holder wasn't quiet about this intent at all.
In January 2014, the United States Department of Justice, in
partnership with the Department of Education, shared the
United States' first national guidelines on school discipline
(George, 2014).

Attorney General Holder and Secretary Duncan advised
schools to stop using suspensions, expulsions, or arrests for
concerns that could be handled more constructively.

Discipline reform advocates praised these efforts. Others railed against them. Opponents of school discipline reform said President Obama's administration was launching a federal war on school discipline (Chavez, 2014). They argued that if Black students were getting harsher punishments than White students for the same infractions, the guidelines should focus exclusively on reducing racial discrimination. Opponents also spun tales of school disciplinary anarchy, stating the Feds believed Black students shouldn't be consequenced for poor behavior. Opponents said the Feds ultimately wanted racial quotas for disciplinary consequences.

Attorney General Holder was unmoved by this sentiment.

The Office of Civil Rights (OCR) under Mr. Holder's leadership investigated a record number of civil rights concerns. In 2015, OCR processed 10,392 complaints about potential civil rights violations at public schools, colleges, and universities ("U.S. Department of Education Releases Report on Office for Civil Rights to Ensure Educational Equity for All Students," 2016). I believe civil rights complaints to OCR skyrocketed during President Obama's administration because the public knew OCR would act on civil rights concerns. The Office of Civil Rights during President Obama's administration released many 'friend of the court' briefs that were not solely related to civil rights violations in schools but also to civil rights violations in general.

In April 2016, OCR reached a settlement with Oklahoma City Public Schools after investigating disproportionate suspension rates of African-American students ("Obama's Civil Rights Divisions," 2016). OCR investigated Fort Bend Independent School District in Texas for the same reason. They investigated school districts in Minneapolis, Mississippi, Kentucky, Chicago, New York City, Iowa, and Washington State. Quite frankly, the Office of Civil Rights had enough of schools systematically jettisoning Black students out of classrooms. These actions were completely in line with OCR's mission.

The OCR was created in 1966 to ensure schools complied with the tenets of Title VI of the Civil Rights Act of 1964. Specifically, OCR was created to prevent discrimination in public education based on race, color, and national origin. Under

Attorney General Holder's leadership, the OCR did what it was founded to do, which was a positive step for public education and the fight against disproportionate suspension and expulsion. The message from the Office of Civil Rights was clear. Schools could not receive federal funds to ensure the free and appropriate public education of all children and still disproportionately suspend and expel Black children out of school.

While the federal government influences policymaking by attaching deliverables to funds they dole out for public education, state legislatures have the most influence over state education policy. It is a state's right to govern public schools and enact policies that benefit a state's students. Still, it is the collective responsibility of citizens to ensure all students have equal protection under the law. Citizens of a state must ensure that all students' civil rights are protected. Citizens must hold their elected officials accountable for ensuring all people are protected under the law. When there is a deficit of care and a lack of policy that ensures students have equal opportunities to benefit from public schooling, legislatures set the stage for schools to sometimes terrorize groups of children.

A deficit of care and policy that ensures equal educational opportunities for all children is how we ended up in the mess we're in now with the disproportionate suspension and expulsion of African-American students. Some folks genuinely believe that African-American students jettisoned from schools for breaking the rules are merely getting what they deserve. I beg to differ. I've worked in some of the toughest schools in several school districts. I've signed off on suspensions and expulsions of students who, in part due to failures of the school districts they were in, were thugs whose infractions warranted the out-of-school consequences they got. That being said, let me be clear. A large number of these suspensions were an 'adult problem,' not a problem with the students or their behavior. Research tells us that in the aggregate, African-American students don't 'act out' any more than White students (Rudd, 2014). So the multitudes of African-American students getting put out of school are not 'getting what they deserve.' They are receiving the brunt of racially disproportionate out-of-school consequences, resulting from a dubious application of school-based discipline policies.

States' legislative responses to the disparate impact of school discipline policies have been lukewarm until recent interest in restorative practices as policy mandates. Still, the legislative foundation for school discipline policy is overwhelmingly reactive. The suspension tends to be most school districts' go-to response for a third of behavior infractions (Fenning & Rose, 2007). Proactive measures, those with the potential to teach students alternative behavior responses, are rarely used—even for non-violent behavior infractions. When one analyzes school districts' codes of conduct across the country, the written documents rely on a brief list of punitive responses dominated by suspensions and expulsions (Fenning & Rose, 2007). There appears to be a chasm in the place where proactive alternatives to address students' misbehavior could and should exist.

References

Adams, J. M. (2015, February 18). *Study: Suspensions harm 'well-behaved' kids*. Retrieved from https://edsource.org/2015/study-suspensions-harm-well-behaved-kids/72501

Center, S. P. L. (2020, May 22). *Georgia board of education reverses Gwinnett County student's expulsion after SPLC intervention*. Retrieved from www.splcenter.org/presscenter/georgia-board-education-reverses-gwinnett-county-students-expulsion-after-splc

Chavez, L. (2014, May 11). *The Federal war on school discipline*. Retrieved from https://nypost.com/2014/01/10/the-federal-war-on-school-discipline/

Copur-Gencturk, Y., Cimpian, J. R., Lubienski, S. T., & Thacker, I. (2020). Teachers' bias against the mathematical ability of female, black, and Hispanic students. *Educational Researcher, 49*(1), 30–43.

de Brey, C., Musu, L., McFarland, J., Wilkinson-Flicker, S., Diliberti, M., Zhang, A., . . . Wang, X. (2019). *Status and trends in the education of racial and ethnic groups 2018*. NCES 2019-038. National Center for Education Statistics.

Fenning, P., & Rose, J. (2007). Overrepresentation of African American students in exclusionary discipline. *Urban Education, 42*(6), 536–559.

George, D. S. (2014, January 8). *Holder, Duncan announce national guidelines on school discipline*. Retrieved from www.washingtonpost.com/local/

education/holder-duncan-announce-national-guidelines-on-school-discipline/2014/01/08/436c5a5e-7899-11e3-8963-b4b654bcc9b2_story.html

Jensen, L. (2020, August 5). *Oregon's Black and indigenous kids are disciplined at twice the rate of their White classmates*. Retrieved from www.wweek.com/news/2020/08/05/oregons-black-and-indigenous-kids-are-disciplined-at-twice-the-rate-of-their-white-classmates/

Obama's civil rights divisions. (2016, April 27). Retrieved from https://politicallyshort.com/2016/04/27/obamas-civil-rights-divisions/

Rudd, T. (2014). *Racial disproportionality in school discipline: Implicit bias is heavily implicated*. Kirwan Institute for the Study of Race and Ethnicity.

Shwe, E. (2020, June 29). *Report shows school suspension and arrest rates remain highest for Black students*. Retrieved from www.marylandmatters.org/2020/06/24/report-shows-school-suspension-and-arrest-rates-remain-highest-for-black-students/

Solis, S. (2020, September 7). *Black girls in Massachusetts 3.9 times more likely to face school discipline, report shows*. Retrieved from www.masslive.com/news/2020/09/in-massachusetts-black-girls-are-39-times-more-likely-to-face-school-discipline-than-white-counterparts-report-shows.html

Staats, C. (2016). Understanding implicit bias: What educators should know. *American Educator, 39*(4), 29.

U.S. department of education releases report on office for civil rights to ensure educational equity for all students. (2016, May 4). Retrieved from www.ed.gov/news/press-releases/us-department-education-releases-report-office-civil-rights-ensure-educational-equity-all-students

Further Readings and Additional References

www.dallasnews.com/news/education/2018/04/05/black-students-still-disciplined-more-often-more-harshly-than-white-peers-report-says/

www.nytimes.com/2012/03/06/education/black-students-face-more-harsh-discipline-data-shows.html

8

Preparing for the Restorative Justice Tribunal

What Is a Restorative Justice Tribunal?

The Restorative Justice Tribunal (the Tribunal) is a forum and process designed to divert students away from out-of-school consequences and restore their standing in a school community. Necessity is the mother of invention, and the Tribunal was born from an urgent need. We needed to stop suspending African-American students five times more frequently than their peers, even though Black students weren't a third of the student population of my school. The lopsided assignment of suspensions and expulsions needed to stop.

A tribunal is defined as a person or institution with authority to adjudicate, pass judgment, or determine claims or disputes. A Restorative Justice Tribunal is a group vested by a school leader with the authority to validate agreements between parties and repair harms that individuals cause in a school community. The Tribunal is comprised of an offending student, a number of Restorative Justice Facilitators, and Restorative Justice Peer Mentors. During a Tribunal meeting, offenders get to tell their story and reflect on their actions. The Restorative Justice Tribunal structure helps students understand how their behavior harmed the community. The Tribunal also helps offenders understand the importance of repairing any harm their actions cause to others.

For the Restorative Justice Tribunal to succeed, several elements were critical. When I launched restorative justice in my school, the two most crucial factors, ironically, had little to do with the urgent need to reduce suspensions and expulsion. As alluded to before, those factors were time and cost.

Critical Factors for Success

In addition to being able to reduce suspensions and expulsion rates, Restorative Justice Tribunals had to be cost-effective and able to sustain any unexpected budget crisis. I had to ensure the Restorative Justice Tribunal wouldn't die if a budget crisis strained our ability to hire Restorative Justice Facilitators. The Tribunals also had to be time-efficient. Because our school historically struggled to get students to pass state-mandated proficiency exams that occurred every spring, it would be at the expense of students' education and my own professional peril for Tribunals to keep students out of classes for extended periods of time. To maximize efficiency, I wanted Tribunals to last no more than 15 minutes from the time an offender walked into the Tribunal space until the Tribunal ended with a restorative justice agreement. While there was a substantial need to keep order in our school, repair harms, and help students learn from their behavioral mistakes, there was a competing urgent need for students to make adequate progress toward mastering state standards. The only way that was going to happen was to keep kids in class and learning as much as possible.

Along with being time and cost-efficient, the Restorative Justice Tribunal had to work. Restorative Justice Tribunals had to demonstrate quantifiable success at diverting students away from out-of-school consequences as there were many critics of restorative practices. There were vocal critics of restorative practices within my school, my school district, and my city. There were more than enough haters with whom restorative practices had to contend. Even the local newspaper joined in on the restorative justice hateration. The local newspaper ran an above-the-fold article with my students' pictures above a headline suggesting restorative practices did not work. There were 'haters' everywhere.

Faced with this opposition, the Restorative Justice Tribunal had to work. We had to be successful at teaching students how to use tools to navigate the social and in-class situations that sometimes triggered poor behavior choices.

Staff the Tribunal for Positive Outcomes

The primary resource required for a Restorative Justice Tribunal is people. A Restorative Justice Tribunal requires two profession-ally trained adults, plus three or four trained Student Peer Advo-cates. While any staff member with an abundance of emotional intelligence *can* facilitate a Tribunal, I believe a licensed, effective school-based counselor, social worker, or psychologist should facilitate. Having a school counselor, social worker, or psycholo-gist facilitate also reduces liability schools may face when attend-ing to students' mental health related needs.

On most campuses, school counselors are best positioned to facilitate Tribunals because of the unique relationship school counselors have with students. Counselors are trained to help students talk through difficult situations and circumstances. Moreover, the professional standards for school counselors require counselors to facilitate the interventions that happen in the Restorative Justice Tribunal model.

The American School Counselor Association (ASCA) Stan-dards state that school counselors are expected to provide short-term counseling to individuals and small groups, refer to school and community resources on behalf of students, and implement instruction aligned to the ASCA *Mindsets and Behaviors for Student Success* in a group and individual settings. The Restorative Justice Tribunal structure allows school counselors to do these things.

While it is ideal for at least one school counselor to be on a school's Restorative Justice Tribunal team, staffing may look different across schools because school funding varies. If a counselor equipped to facilitate Tribunals is not available, the expertise of social workers and school psychologists serve as excellent choices to be Tribunal Facilitators. Social workers and school psychologists, like school counselors, are trained to support students through discussions. I launched the Restorative Justice Tribunal with a school counselor and a social worker. They anchored the program and provided a balance of skills and approaches.

It is an understatement to say the caseload demands of school social workers, school counselors, and school psychologists are overwhelming. The mental health needs of students are increasing. That demand for mental health services greatly affects the work of these professionals. Schools planning to include school counselors, social workers, or school psychologists in restorative justice solutions should be prepared to adjust these professionals' workloads to accommodate the added responsibility of hearing Tribunal cases. This is especially true in the initial stages of running Tribunals or any other restorative justice intervention.

In my own experience, I reduced the caseload of one school counselor to ensure she had time to attend to her counseling duties and accommodate the responsibilities of the Restorative Justice Tribunal. There will always be competing interests and competing needs in schools that must be reconciled. By analyzing resources available, a school leader will have to identify suitable professionals to participate in restorative justice programming. Whoever is selected must have an abundance of emotional intelligence, a gift for connecting with people, and the ability to train students to be vital Tribunal members.

The Secret Sauce: Restorative Justice Peer Advocates

After identifying the adults to participate on the Restorative Justice Tribunal, there will be a need to identify students to serve on the Tribunal as Restorative Justice Peer Advocates. These Peer

Advocates serve a different purpose than students who partici-pate in a Trial by Peers or Youth Court program. In Trial by Peers, peer members hear a case, pass judgment on an offender, and sentence them to a consequence. What Restorative Justice Peer Advocates do is different. Restorative Justice Tribunal Peer Advocates serve as support persons for offenders during (and often after) Tribunal proceedings. Peer Advocates help partici-pants relax and feel comfortable during the Tribunal proceeding, providing a valuable system of support in an unfamiliar setting.

Restorative Justice Peer Advocates also provide Restorative Justice Tribunal Facilitators with student perspectives on how offenders should repair the harms that arise in Tribunal proceed-ings. Peer Advocates also validate solutions to repair harms that offenders propose during Tribunals. Peer Advocates' presence ensures that students' voices are heard and repatriations are fair and relevant.

It is essential to select the right students to be Restorative Justice Tribunal Peer Advocates, especially when starting the program. When selecting students to be Peer Advocates for the launch of a Tribunal program, first decide when the Restorative Justice Tribunal will convene and identify students for whom the Tribunal fits into their instructional day. This may be differ-ent in elementary schools where master schedulers may have flexibility over when students take special classes and attend scheduled activities. Special classes, activities, and sometimes recess periods may be able to be scheduled to coincide with times a Restorative Justice Tribunal convenes.

In secondary schools, master schedulers can choose to select Peer Advocates from elective classes, create a restorative justice elective class, identify students who have open periods in their schedule, or draw from students who have 'Office Practice' or similar classes in their schedules. The Peer Advocate selection process will look different at each school as well as look differ-ent at the elementary, middle, and high school levels.

Selecting the right students to train as Peer Advocates will help your Restorative Justice Tribunal succeed. When we selected our first cohort of Restorative Justice Tribunal Peer Advocates, we chose students without extreme behavior offenses on their student records and those with good attendance records. We also selected students whom we believed would pay proper attention to confidentiality.

Confidentiality and Training Tribunal Peer Advocates

We selected 30 students to train as Restorative Justice Peer Advocates. With that number of students, I knew we had to impress upon them that confidentiality was essential. We couldn't have students spreading each other's business all over campus. Offenders' confidentiality needed not to be breached because breaches of confidentiality would have, most likely, unraveled the program and the community's confidence in it. The Restorative Justice Peer Advocates training focused heavily on confidentiality.

My school is in 'the neighborhood,' and we had the benefit of many of our students growing up in homes where families impressed upon them, "Don't go out there telling our family business." Most of our students instinctively understood the importance of confidentiality. Still, Tribunal Facilitators emphasized the importance of confidentiality throughout the training. Fortunately, privacy has never been a problem in the years we have run this school-based restorative justice model.

After the Peer Advocate training, we ended up with a gender and racially diverse corps of Peer Advocates. Out of that initial corps of students, those that demonstrated the most eagerness and motivation to be involved were the students we asked to be the inaugural Tribunal Peer Advocates. We knew the corps of Peer Advocates would grow because, by design, the Tribunal invites students who enter as offenders to be trained as Peer Advocates. This further diversified the corps of Peer Advocates and added Peer Advocates with personal investment and 'insider' experiences to the Tribunal Peer Advocate corps.

During the training, we explained to the students why we started a restorative justice program, specifically the importance of reducing suspensions and expulsions. Trainers described how offending students are referred to the Tribunal and Restorative Justice Circles. Trainers modeled what happens in a Restorative Justice Tribunal and a Restorative Justice Circle. They summarized the guidance lessons offenders must take after a Tribunal. The training ended with a detailed discussion about confidentiality. We kept the training under an hour and provided enough time for students to watch a mock Restorative Justice Tribunal and practice being a Tribunal Peer Advocate. After the first year of the program, we ended Tribunal Peer Advocate training with an overview of the program's fantastic success rate to get students to see that the Restorative Justice Tribunal was a worthy cause and they were being asked to join a winning team.

The trainings would conclude, and Facilitators would ask trainees if they would like to take permission slips home to their parents or guardians to become Restorative Justice Peer Advocates. We understood that some parents would not want their children to participate. We understood that some families may not want their children exposed to the behavioral issues of their peers, particularly in such a tough school. Some Tribunal Peer Advocate trainees wanted no part of the Tribunal, and that was fine. The role of Peer Advocate is not for everyone. For other students, participating in the program as Peer Advocates positively changed their lives. We knew the Tribunals were needed, and we suspected the idea would take root in the community. We could not have predicted the success Tribunals would have in affecting students and their maturity.

One school year, Ms. Green mentioned that one of our former students wanted to talk to me. Students dropping by to see me was not uncommon, and my response to Ms. Green was always, "Cool. Let me know when they're coming in." One day, a student named Adrianna walked into my office, but she wasn't the young lady I remembered.

When I first met her, Adrianna wasn't living up to her potential. Frequently body-shamed by her peers for being overweight, Adrianna would lash out and get into fights (that she usually won). Her winning fight-record wound her up in the Deans' Office often. There she established a friendship with the Deans' Office secretaries, who took her under their wings. The ladies kept Adrianna busy and out of trouble by keeping her involved in searches for college scholarships. The secretaries also ensured Adrianna was enrolled in Honors and Advanced Placement classes, regardless if she wanted them or not. They also kept her involved in school activities. They ultimately referred Adrianna to Ms. Green to be a Restorative Justice Peer Advocate.

As a Peer Advocate, Adrianna had an incredible ability to relate to offenders due to her own experiences and history of prize-fighting on campus. She quickly became a core part of the Restorative Justice Tribunal team. She acted as an unofficial mentor to several troubled students on campus. She would tell them, "If I see you on campus acting up, we gon' talk." She also coined the phrase, "If you havin' a bad day, look for me."

Since her own freshman year had been so challenging, Adrianna was a champion for younger students. Peer mentoring evolved into an important—though unofficial—aspect of the restorative justice program, especially since most of the offenders were ninth-grade students.

Now Adriana stood in my office as an adult attending college and finding her way in life. This was Restorative Justice Tribunal Peer Advocate Adrianna. I had to hold it together when she said, "Thank you for allowing me to be a part of the restorative justice program. It's why I decided to study social work in college. I have to do an internship soon. Would you be okay if I did my internship here and worked with the restorative justice program?"

Even today, reflecting on this story makes me a little emotional and very, very proud.

I Had to See My Attorney

In the earliest stages of planning to launch the Restorative Justice Tribunal, I checked in with my district's Legal Department. The last thing I wanted was to wind up in my supervisor's office by making a legal misstep while trying to do right by children. The primary concern was that of student confidentiality. I needed the Legal Department's advice on whether getting permission from offenders' parents was sufficient to allow Peer Advocates to hear details of offenders' disciplinary incidents. These details are confidential, and I didn't want to violate the Family Education Rights and Privacy Act (FERPA).

My students needed every advantage in life they could get. I didn't want unnecessary out-of-school consequences to derail them from pursuing goals and dreams. I didn't want any avoidable setbacks to the program's success. Therefore, the legal advice was crucial in examining the approach the Tribunal would be taking. Ultimately, the Legal Department confirmed that if parents permitted students to participate, the program would be on a solid legal footing. We were good to go.

Cross-checking every facet of the program was crucial, particularly because I was one of only three Black high school principals in my entire state. Managing that stress and scrutiny was hard enough. When my Caucasian peers made mistakes, they were just that—easily resolved missteps. Allies often shared with me the private conversations they had with my White peers and supervisors, scrutinizing my leadership decisions and those of other African-American leaders. It was clear that mistakes made by African-American principals were regarded as statements about the competence of *all* Black principals (and *all* Black employees). This perspective was ridiculous but not surprising to me. While Nevada is known as 'The Silver State,' Black Nevadans sometimes assign another identifier to describe their collective experience—'The Mississippi of the West.'

The 'Mississippi of the West' label began after *Ebony* magazine published an article by James Goodrich in March 1954 titled, "Negroes can't win in Las Vegas" ("'Mississippi of the West' in 1954 Magazine's scathing article turned heads in Las Vegas," 1999). The article analyzed the Jim Crow nature of Las Vegas. Goodrich wrote, "Las Vegas, the fabulous gambling and resort spa . . . is rigidly Jim Crow by custom. No other town outside of Dixie has more racial barriers" ("'Mississippi of the West' in 1954 Magazine's scathing article turned heads in Las Vegas," 1999).

This historic article chronicled discrimination, employment, and living conditions for Black Las Vegans in the 1950s:

> The Negro finds little welcome anywhere. He is barred from practically every place whites go for entertainment or services. He cannot live outside a segregated, slum-like community. He is relegated to the most menial jobs. For the Negro, Vegas is as bad as towns come. . . . Negroes rate no better than second-class citizenship there.
>
> ("'Mississippi of the West' in 1954 Magazine's scathing article turned heads in Las Vegas," 1999)

Adding insight into housing and segregation in Las Vegas in 1954, Goodrich wrote,

"Negroes of Las Vegas have more to worry about than the gamblers. Housing is their most immediate problem. They presently live 'across the tracks' in a segregated, unkept area covering about 10 square blocks on the city's west flank. Called Westside, the site is separated from white communities by a yard of railroad tracks and a pedestrian-auto underpass which Negroes jokingly refer to as the 'Iron Curtain.'" ("'Mississippi of the West' in 1954 Magazine's scathing article turned heads in Las Vegas," 1999).

The 'iron curtain' still exists in Las Vegas. The underpass is still there. The Westside continues to be segregated, and business investment and development on the Westside lags behind much of the city. The job market in the Las Vegas Valley remains Jim Crow-esque for African-Americans. Unemployment rates for African-Americans in Nevada exceeded 10% in 2007 and was the highest unemployment rate for African-Americans among many large metropolitan areas (Austin, 2012). In 2010, African-American unemployment in Las Vegas was comparable to unemployment rates during the Great Depression (Austin, 2011). African-American unemployment reached 22.6% in 2011 and dropped to 15% in 2014 (Christiansen, 2015). By comparison, during this time, the unemployment rate was 7.6% for White people and 7.8% for Hispanics (Christiansen, 2015).

The metaphorical 'iron curtain' for Black Las Vegans has evolved into a seemingly omnipresent barrier that separates

African-American Las Vegans from access to opportunities. This 'Iron Curtain' phenomenon isn't exclusive to Las Vegas. These sorts of barriers exist in many major cities. Go to 'the hood' in most major metropolitan cities, and many residents will be able to tell you which physical structures are regarded as the lines of demarcation that separate them from the rest of their city. These tangible structures represent the proverbial barrier that separates them from opportunities others in their city seem to have.

This insidious bias underpinned the perspectives some folks would form about my decisions as principal as well as the outcomes my students hoped to achieve. Laying the correct foundations for the restorative justice program was crucial to protect ourselves from potential attacks. Legal advice was a critical component of that foundation.

The Discipline Playbook and Tribunal Workflow

For the Restorative Justice Tribunal to work, we had to be clear on the workflow. We had to know the steps involved for a student to get from a classroom to the Restorative Justice Tribunal. The workflow had to be systematic, written down, and predictable so that program structures could be monitored, evaluated, and improved as time went on.

School districts and charter organizations typically have a district-level Code of Conduct that governs how schools assign consequences when students commit behavioral infractions. That Code of Conduct is usually a long, legal document steeped in policy and anchored in state laws and administrative codes. School-based staff distill these documents or policy statements into manageable shorthand versions, which are much more end-user friendly. The shortened versions function as the standard operating procedure for administering discipline at the school level. This path is how federal and state law typically becomes school district policy and regulations, which leads to school-level procedures.

The shorthand guide is usually written in an 'action equals consequence' manner, which instructs staff to do 'this' if the student does 'that.' Furthermore, the frequency of a behavior is usually a factor in these shorthand guides. So if a student has been consequenced for doing 'this' behavior 'X' number of times, then 'that' would be the appropriate response. If school-based personnel govern their actions in alignment with these guides, they remain in alignment with their district policy and with their respective state laws. By sticking to the guide, they should also maintain an equitable approach to assigning disciplinary consequences to students. In this school-based version of disciplinary procedures, a school identifies the behavior infractions that trigger a restorative response, rather than a punishment or out-of-school consequence. The process of referring a student to a school's restorative justice program should be identical to the process a school uses to respond to poor behavior choices—up until a student is ready to be assigned a consequence.

At that point, a student should be diverted from a potential out-of-school consequence and assigned a restorative response. To be concrete, the process may look something like this:

1. Jeff is in class and makes a poor behavior choice.
2. The situation in class escalates, and Jeff's teacher has Jeff removed from class and escorted to an administrator.
3. Jeff is escorted to an administrator, and upon Jeff's arrival, the office staff asks Jeff to write a statement about the incident, affording Jeff due process and allowing him to reflect and decompress.
4. While Jeff completes his statement, a referral from the teacher makes it to the administrator that Jeff is about to see.
5. When Jeff meets with the administrator, that administrator reviews Jeff's behavior history, notices he has been in trouble multiple times, and sees Jeff is due for an out-of-school consequence according to established school procedures.
6. The administrator reviews the referral and Jeff's witness statement and talks with Jeff about the incident. The administrator finds Jeff's behavior to be inappropriate

and an irritant but not an egregious violation of the school's code of discipline.

If the school did *not* have a restorative justice program in place, the administrator would suspend Jeff for some number of days. However, because the school has a restorative justice program, the administrator would recommend Jeff to a Restorative Justice Tribunal, which keeps Jeff in school. Instead of generating suspension paperwork, the administrator prints a permission slip for Jeff's family to approve participation in the school's Restorative Justice Tribunal program. Schools with restorative justice programming divert students from suspension to other pathways that keep students in school.

Once a school assigns a student to restorative justice, the administrator should call home to inform the student's parent or guardian of the incident. The administrator should make a proposal to the offender's family that the student participates in the restorative justice program instead of being given an out-of-school behavioral consequence. The administrator must clearly communicate the benefits of restorative justice with the offender's family. The administrator must explain that restorative justice helps students reflect on behavior, keeps them in school, and helps them avoid making the same missteps in the future.

The administrator must also inform the student's parent or guardian that the school will require a signed permission slip for their student to participate because they will share details of their behavior incident with a group of their peers and adults. Finally, the administrator must explain that if the permission slip is not immediately returned, the school must proceed with regular school discipline, which would be an out-of-school behavioral consequence.

If the parent or guardian agrees, then the administrator will send a permission slip home with the student. Once the permission slip is returned, the witness statements and a copy of the referral should be sent to the restorative justice personnel who schedules students for the Restorative Justice Tribunal or Restorative Justice Circle, depending on the infraction.

Sometimes Kids Should Be Given Consequences

Every intervention will not work for every child, and the same is true of restorative practices and the Restorative Justice Tribunal. In my experience, I only allowed a student to enter our restorative justice program twice in a school year. If the program is working for that student, then they should not commit any more serious infractions that would place them on the pathway for suspension more than twice in a school year. Everyone makes mistakes. I understand that. Also, unfortunate things can sometimes happen to good people. That's understandable too. Still, I decided that students could only go through our restorative justice program structures twice in a school year. I didn't want to give students anything that remotely looked like unlimited passes from consequences for naughty behavior.

Most teachers on my staff understood the challenges our students brought with them to school and were patient, understanding, and supportive—the picture of 'warm demandingness.' My district has over 50 high schools, and my school is widely regarded as one of the three toughest high schools in the city. Educators know that boundaries are important. Boundaries are especially important at my school.

My thought process was this: if a student needed to be diverted from out-of-school consequences more than twice in a school year, then they were choosing not to respond to the socioemotional supports we put in place through the Restorative Justice Tribunal and the restorative justice program. Those supports were in addition to the abundance of support structures my school offered outside of the restorative justice program. If students continued to 'act up,' we needed to try something different, and that wouldn't be a third opportunity to go through the Restorative Justice Tribunal.

In addition to repairing the harm through a Tribunal proceeding, students also had to participate in guidance lessons designed to teach them strategies to steer clear of any influences that might prompt them to engage in the behaviors that landed them in the Tribunal in the first place. We wanted to prevent students from being 'frequent fliers' in administrators' offices.

Let me talk for a moment about 'frequent fliers.' Sometimes school personnel believe that students frequently referred for behavioral infractions should not be afforded the opportunity to participate in a school's restorative justice structures, regardless if it is their first infraction in a school year. Sometimes students can be intensely disrespectful to staff members, and the perception (real or not) is that they (and their home environments) are not responsive to the school's frequent requests for support. With these students, school staff sometimes throw up their hands, declaring that restorative justice structures are not for them. I emphatically disagree with that sentiment. In my experience, these are often the students that benefit the most from restorative justice structures. Sometimes it is the wraparound supports offered through restorative justice that will redirect that troubled student and prevent them from engaging in increasingly problematic behavior. In my opinion, it is better to try and fail than not try at all.

References

Austin, A. (2011, October 3). *High black unemployment widespread across nation's metropolitan areas*. Economic Policy Institute.

Austin, A. (2012, July 2). *Black metropolitan unemployment in 2011*. Economic Policy Institute.

Christiansen, R. (2015, January 30). *Is the black middle class disappearing in Las Vegas?* Retrieved from https://knpr.org/knpr/2015-01/black-middle-class-disappearing-las-vegas

'Mississippi of the West' in 1954 Magazine's scathing article turned heads in Las Vegas. (1999, March 21). Retrieved from https://lasvegassun.com/news/1999/mar/21/mississippi-of-the-west-in-1954-magazines-scathing/

9

Running the Restorative Justice Tribunal

Ms. Green had been designated as a restorative practice trainer for our entire school district. She was preparing to host a large group of observers who wanted to see how to run Restorative Justice Tribunals and know how to reduce suspensions and expulsions. Ms. Green had all the case files organized and prepared. She had already prepared the Restorative Justice Peer Advocates to let them know there would be guest observers on campus. She had already consulted with my secretary to ensure I had time on my schedule to visit the observers and answer questions they may have. When the day began, Ms. Green was prepared to be the perfect host and ambassador for the program.

Ms. Green came into my office later that morning, visibly rattled. Ms. Green is a very tall, confident, wonderful person. She reminds me of a power forward for a professional women's basketball team, unquestionably physically formidable. In this instance in my office though, she was shaken, and her face was ashen. Clearly, something was wrong.

"None of them have been here today! We have a room of eight people waiting to see cases, and the last four students I've gone to get have been absent!"

Retrieving the Offender

To launch the Tribunal, Restorative Justice Facilitators must first retrieve the offending student who has been referred to the program. This may be deceptively more difficult than it seems. In my experience, some students who are referred to the Tribunal sometimes have attendance challenges. My school is a demonstration school and training center for restorative practices, so it is common to have guests in the building to observe the day's schedule of Restorative Justice Tribunals and Restorative Justice Circles. I remember quite a few days when Ms. Green would come to me visibly frustrated when students on the docket for the day were all absent.

This happens, so it's essential to be prepared. It is important for the administrator to allocate five or six cases on the days that Tribunals and Circles are scheduled to be observed. This ensures that time is not wasted and increases the likelihood that guests are able to observe Tribunals.

Another factor to be mindful of is choosing who is sent to retrieve students scheduled to participate in restorative justice programming from their classes. I remember sitting in a biweekly restorative justice meeting early in the life of our program. We were discussing workflow—a standard agenda item for these meetings. A thought struck me, and I asked, "Who are you sending to get offenders from class?"

The team responded, "Student aides," and my stomach dropped. Some of the students that appeared before the Tribunal were the most behaviorally volatile students in my school, so sending other students to escort them to the Tribunal space risked creating situations where new behavior infractions might occur. Also, student aides do not command the respect of teachers who may be resistant to restorative justice.

Student aides' role is to perform clerical tasks and deliver hall passes to teachers. Sometimes, student aides would give teachers a pass from Restorative Justice Facilitators for an offender to report to the Tribunal, but the teacher would decide that they needed to cover more points in their lesson before excusing the summoned student to the Tribunal. Sometimes, teachers would get so caught up in teaching, they would forget about the hall pass altogether. Some teachers who did not agree with the principles of restorative practices, especially when we first launched the restorative justice program, didn't release students to report to the Tribunal at all as an act of passive resistance to restorative justice. For these reasons, it is important to have an adult retrieve students to attend Tribunals.

Having an adult retrieve offenders from their classes serves multiple purposes. While on the way to the Tribunal from the offender's class, the adult can make small talk with the student and outline how the Tribunal operates and what the student should expect. The goal of the conversation during the walk to the Tribunal space is to make the experience predictable, give them an 'advanced organizer,' and to help the offender be comfortable when the Tribunal begins.

Setup

Before the Tribunal starts, the Restorative Justice Facilitators brief Peer Advocates on the cases of the day. The Facilitators remind Peer Advocates of the importance of confidentiality and answer any questions Peer Advocates may have about the Restorative Justice Tribunal process.

Get Everyone to the Tribunal Table

A Tribunal has a standard composition and process of operation. There are usually three to four Restorative Justice Peer Advocates present in the Tribunal space, an adult who records the minutes for the meeting, plus the Restorative Justice Tribunal Facilitator who runs the meeting. Everything should happen in an office space that is warm and inviting for the students. This space must also be secure enough to protect offenders' confidentiality and protect them from shame.

The First of Five Key Questions

The Tribunal begins with warm introductions of everyone in the Tribunal space and another overview of what will occur in the Tribunal. Again, the goal is to make the Tribunal experience predictable and comfortable for the offender. Next, the Restorative Justice Facilitator begins the Tribunal by asking the offender a series of questions. The Tribunal is anchored by a few powerful questions that drive reflection, empathy, and actions in students, teachers, and the school at large.

The five questions asked in the Tribunal are:

◆   The 'question of the day.'
◆   What happened?
◆   What are the effects of what happened on you and others?
◆   What is your responsibility to make the school community a better place?
◆   What's the solution to repair the harm?

The first question is known as the 'question of the day.' It is an icebreaker that humanizes all participants in the Tribunal space and allows everyone in the room to get to know each other better. When I train people to run Tribunals, I get some pretty comical inquiries about the 'question of the day.'

Let me clear a few things up. There are no secret, magical questions of the day. The questions of the day are not proprietary. They are open-ended questions to encourage thought and explanation. Everyone in the room must answer the question to reduce the intensity of the focus on the offending student. Restorative Justice Facilitators ask questions (of the day) such as:

◆   Who is your favorite role model and why?
◆   What worries you about aging, if anything?
◆   What is your favorite dessert to eat on the weekend, and why?

Another reason why the 'question of the day' is important is because the offender in the Tribunal may not know or have a relationship with the Facilitators, and it is best to do as much as we can to make the offenders comfortable enough to communicate openly. Offenders may have seen the Restorative Justice Facilitators around campus, but they may not have a relationship with them. While answering one question in the Tribunal space does not constitute a relationship, the shared experience among participants is the start of a connection with the adult Restorative Justice Facilitators and with the Peer Advocates.

I have known students to enter this structure as Restorative Justice Tribunal offenders and exit with the foundations of genuine friendships with the Peer Advocates. Because the human brain does not process information as well when it is in a state of panic or fear, helping students relax via the 'question of the day' is not simply a secondary outcome or an afterthought. It's essential. The question of the day sets the tone for the rest of the Tribunal process. Opening with a non-threatening question switches students' brains on to the reflective nature of the Restorative Justice Tribunal process and lowers their stress levels.

Since a Restorative Justice Tribunal is assigned in lieu of discipline, it is common for students to project any fears they may have and anxieties they associate with disciplinary procedures onto the experience of the Tribunal. While it may be impossible to completely allay students' fears, the question of the day helps put Restorative Justice Tribunal offenders' minds at ease. It is much more effective than if Restorative Justice Facilitators began by asking offenders about the incident that got them referred to the Tribunal. Starting by asking offenders about their respective behavior incidents would place most students into a defensive frame of mind.

The Second Key Question

After all the participants in the Restorative Justice Tribunal answer the 'question of the day,' the Restorative Justice Facilitator allows offenders to tell their side of the story about the incident that occurred. The next question Facilitators ask offenders is, "What happened?"

Year after year, time after time, program evaluation after program evaluation, participants tell us the same thing. What they appreciate the most from participating in the Restorative Justice Tribunal is being able to tell their story and being heard by the adults in the school and their peers. Think about it; when a student goes to see a school disciplinarian, they are heard but often only as far as due process goes. And this telling is often overshadowed by the report received from the teacher, the student's disciplinary history, plus whatever distractions the disciplinarian is experiencing in that moment.

In the Restorative Justice Tribunal, the student's story drives the process. A student tells their story to an administrator, two licensed personnel, and a group of their peers and for a different purpose—to repair any harm their behavior caused. Admittedly, when students sit down in the chair reserved for offenders, they may not completely understand this. They may have difficulty seeing how their actions affected others.

Perhaps it is the fact that Tribunals last up to 15 minutes and are free from distractions, while visits to administrators for disciplinary reasons can be much shorter. Maybe the behavior infractions that get referred to Restorative Justice Tribunals are those that more easily generate conversation and perspective-taking when one explores 'what happened.' Or maybe the adrenaline and emotional state a student experiences when they are confronted with out-of-school consequences make it more difficult to recognize they are being heard when an administrator asks them 'what happened' when deciding whether or not to issue them disciplinary consequences. Whatever the reason, students overwhelmingly report they feel genuinely heard when they share 'what happened' in the Restorative Justice Tribunal space.

The Third and Fourth Key Questions

After offenders tell their story, Restorative Justice Facilitators ask them to reflect and to identify what prompted the behavior that caused harm to the teacher, a peer, the class community, or to the school community at large. This is done by asking offenders the next question in the Tribunal process: "What are the effects of what happened on you and on others?"

Self-analysis, self-reflection, and empathy matter, and all are an integral part of this school-based restorative justice model. The point of this question is to get a student offender to not only process the behavior that occurred but also see how their behavior impacted them and affected others around them.

In the years we have spent perfecting this Tribunal model, we have found that even our most challenging students have an extremely powerful sense of responsibility for how their actions impact their peers. Peer group acceptance means so much to students, so this question—when asked in front of the Peer Advocates and in this process—takes on a whole new light and yields a restorative result.

This happened during the Tribunal for a student named Danya who came to school dressed in the most beautiful skirt and blouse ensemble. She was the picture of style the day she walked through the halls to class in that ensemble. The problem was Danya's stylish outfit was far too risqué for school. Ms. Gerda saw that Danya's skirt was missing, give or take, eight inches of fabric before it could even start being considered as appropriate for school. Ms. Gerda told Danya she was out of dress code because her skirt was too short, and Danya erupted on Ms. Gerda. Danya told Ms. Gerda she had no right questioning her clothes. Danya yelled that she had been to three classes already that day, and her other teachers didn't say anything about her skirt being too short. Danya told Ms. Gerda that Ms. Gerda needed to mind her business. A crowd had formed. The event had become a spectacle. But Ms. Gerda would not be moved. Unphased, Ms. Gerda sternly directed Danya to report to the Deans' Office because her skirt was too short and out of dress code. Danya ignored Ms. Gerda, called her a "Bitch," and walked away. Ms. Gerda referred Danya to the Deans' Office for profanity and insubordination.

When the Deans' Office got the case, a Dean referred Danya to Restorative Justice. And it was in the Tribunal that Danya acknowledged her actions impacted others, especially Ms.

Gerda. After having time to reflect on her behavior, Danya realized she could have handled her conflict with Ms. Gerda differently. Danya was an extremely bright young lady who knew
many more words than the ugly ones she used to scream at
Ms. Gerda about her short skirt. In the Restorative Justice Post
Conference—and we'll discuss Post Conferences later in this
book—Danya told Ms. Gerda that she realized she embarrassed
her and that she was sorry for her actions. Dayna told
Ms. Gerda, "I'm so sorry, Ms. Gerda. I know you were just
doing your job when you dress coded me. You didn't deserve
all that. I'm so, so sorry. I made us both look bad." It was a
precious moment.

Once an offender has told the Tribunal what happened and
reflected on the effects of their behavior, the next question the
Facilitator asks is, "What is your responsibility to make the
school community better?" In the Restorative Justice Tribunal
process, it is important to help students see they are individuals
whose behavior impacts an entire group. The students who gave
me advice about what needed to be in our approach to restorative justice were insistent on this, and they were right. In this
era where standing out because 'likes' on social media provide
social currency, schools must be intentional in the way they help
students see they are individual members of a larger community
and their treatment of school community members matters.

While it may be cool for students to appear aloof, students
understand the concept of being careful not to behave in ways
to embarrass others, particularly their family unit. With inten-
tionality schools must help students to see their classroom community as a unit or their grade level as a unit or their school as
a unit. Let me be clear though; this is not always an easy understanding to help students develop, and some students may not
buy into this at all. After all, in some school districts, teachers
may not model a commitment to the community since teachers
transfer among schools frequently. Still, it is important to get
students to understand how their behavior impacts the school
community. This understanding creates the conditions for whole-
school change as it relates to behaviors that facilitate academic
success for all students.

The Final Key Question and the Search for Solutions

The final question the Restorative Justice Tribunal Facilitators ask offenders is, "What's the solution to repair the harm done in this situation?" This is the moment an offender can recommend to the Tribunal how they can repair the harm their behavior has caused. Restorative Justice Facilitators should have a number of solutions they are prepared to recommend to offenders that are appropriate for the school and population they serve. This takes some of the pressure off the offender to come up with solutions and provides examples for offenders to see what kind of agreements and actions are appropriate to repair a harm.

For instance, some solutions we have used are:

♦ A supervised lunch with the other party, whether they are a student or teacher;
♦ Mandatory tutoring if the Tribunal panel believes the root of the harm is academic;
♦ Campus cleanup; and
♦ An apology letter to be read to the individual or to the class. A Restorative Justice Facilitator must approve the draft apology letter before it is presented to the party that was harmed.

And that's just to name a few. Whatever works for your school's population should be ready to implement at the conclusion of the Tribunal; however, I advise schools to remain open to solutions that school leaders and the Tribunal Facilitators have not considered.

Besides these solutions, the offender might provide an ingenious solution that the Tribunal would never have come up with. The more a student can own their solution, the more likely the behavioral problem will be successfully resolved.

When this happens, the Restorative Justice Facilitators should give the solution a preliminary approval (if it is plausible) and an administrator should quickly provide the final approval.

This happened when a student named Ardene had a Restorative Justice Tribunal for talking back and being insubordinate to Ms. Kinney, one of her teachers. She told the Tribunal she was disrespectful to Ms. Kinney because she was tired and irritable. Ms. Green asked,

> "Are you tired because you are staying up late at night . . . doing homework? Watching TV? Talking on the phone?"

Nobody was ready for Ardene's explanation.

> "Me and six of my girls have been sneaking out of the house late at night to meet up with six freshman boys. We're starting a gang."

That statement sucked the oxygen out of the room. Ardene, her girlfriends, and six boys had been sneaking out of their homes in the middle of the night to meet in the desert to participate in gang initiation activities. Ardene said she was sneaking out and participating in the gang activities because she wanted to prove to her friends that she 'belonged' to the group. Ardene's Tribunal case took on a new light at that point. Ardene had to repair the harm to Ms. Kinney, yes. But the Tribunal now had to resolve the more pressing concern of Ardene placing herself in danger. The Tribunal also had a confidentiality issue: because she was in danger, Ms. Green had to inform Ardene's parents of what she was doing.

Ardene came up with the solution. She decided to dissolve the gang and stop all its activities. It turned out that Ardene was not just a member of the gang that was forming. She was a leader. She also pledged to tell her father about her behavior because she knew if she did not, Ms. Green would. Ms. Green and Coach Esaw gave Ardene until the end of the school day to tell her father about the group she was forming.

Ms. Green and Coach Esaw told the Deans' Office the names of all the students who were participating in the gang activities. They also called Ardene's father and told him about the group she had formed, but as Ardene promised, she had already told him. The next day, Ardene's dad came to Cheyenne to meet and thank Ms. Green and Coach Esaw.

He said, "Thank you so much for helping me figure out what was going on with my daughter."

It was a beautiful moment for everyone.

Now Ardene is thriving. She has a new set of friends and is academically successful. In her Tribunal experience she came up with a unique solution that put her life on a different, better, infinitely more positive path.

Admittedly, it is rare for an offender to come up with a solution that is not already on the list of solutions that has evolved over time. Still, it is important that the Tribunal panel (and the entire process) is pliable enough to incorporate new ideas.

Deliberation and Additional Tools

After the offender proposes a solution to the Tribunal or agrees to a solution that has been proposed to them, one of the Restorative Justice Facilitators then escorts the student into another room to reflect on the proceedings while the panel and a facilitator deliberate. This is the beauty of having a school counselor, school social worker, or school psychologist as one of the Facilitators. When the adult and the offender are alone, the facilitator can engage in a more therapeutic discussion with the student.

The person who escorts the student to a room while the panel deliberates can help the offender process the events of the Tribunal, continue to help them process the impact of their behavior on themselves and others, and immediately respond to any emotional difficulty or distress the offender may experience. At the end of the panel's deliberation, the agreed upon solution is recorded on a Restorative Justice Tribunal Agreement Form. All parties in the Tribunal sign the form. The Tribunal Facilitators then ensure that the offender follows through with the proposed solutions promptly. If the offender does not follow through with the agreed upon solution, the case should be referred back to the administrator and to the regular disciplinary process.

Besides a solution, the Restorative Justice Tribunal process has to end with the student developing tools that will help them learn what to do if confronted again with the circumstances that got them referred to the Restorative Justice Tribunal. Every student referred to the Tribunal must participate in a guidance lesson. We use various guidance lessons to facilitate this. Most of the socioemotional learning curricula on the market is rather good. Even if these curricula don't fully meet the needs of a school population, they are a fantastic starting point for guidance lessons. A skilled guidance counselor, social worker, or school psychologist can take most socioemotional learning 'canned curriculum' and make it work for their students. Facilitators use the guidance lessons to help offenders identify and address the root of the student's behavior.

In my experience, it is the combination of approaches that create a complete solution: helping students be empathetic to whomever their behavior has harmed, seeing how their behavior impacts others in the community, seeking forgiveness, and receiving socioemotional skills (via guidance lessons). I believe this is why, in my experience, students who have gone through the Restorative Justice Tribunal process rarely end up back in the Deans' Office. Our restorative justice program has had a 98% success rate over the last seven years, which I attribute to this enabling formula.

10

After the Restorative Justice Tribunal

Charlie joined a gang. However, this was not the typical street gang with whom we were accustomed to dealing. This was a crime syndicate. The organization had members all over North and South America, and Charlie was desperate for membership and the feeling of belonging that membership would provide. They jumped Charlie in; however, when they jumped him in, the gang members didn't know that 'he' was really a 'she.' Charlie was transgender, had changed his mind about membership in the gang, and he knew he would be killed if he tried to get out. Charlie knew their retribution would be particularly fierce not only for trying to leave the gang but also for deceiving them about being transgender. Charlie disclosed this information to Ms. Green while Coach Esaw and the Restorative Justice Peer Advocates were deliberating. Ultimately, we had to connect Charlie with resources to get him out of that situation. This is the kind of support we've given to students through the Restorative Justice Tribunal process. Stories and needs surface when the door to enter the Tribunal space was closed, while the Tribunal Facilitators and Peer Advocates, or during follow-up visits between offenders and Restorative Justice Facilitators. When the door closes for RJ deliberation, the counseling and support doesn't stop. Every moment of the Restorative Justice Tribunal experience is purposeful.

The Tribunal Process Sometimes Uncovers Things

The Tribunal process sometimes uncovers things that interrupt a student's ability to succeed at school or that disrupt a student's ability to engage in normal functions of life. After the Tribunal concludes for the day, the Facilitators can connect with students for further counseling if further counseling support is necessary. Restorative Justice Facilitators may refer students to psychological services or other wraparound supports in or outside of school.

We've connected entire families to resources necessary to ensure students were able to function academically and emotionally. Through the Tribunal process, we have identified families whose basic human needs were unmet for extended periods of time. We've identified kids who were deeply angry because they were hungry or because the lights were turned off in their homes or there was no heat in their houses or air-conditioning, a necessity when living in Las Vegas.

Restorative Post Conferences With Teachers

After a day of Restorative Justice Tribunals is concluded and solutions to repair harms are proposed and agreed upon, the Facilitators schedule Restorative Justice Post Conferences. Post Conferences involve Facilitators and teachers who referred students to administration for violations of the Code of Conduct. The Restorative Justice Post Conference is an essential part of this school-based restorative justice model. One premise of this model of behavior management is that adults have the most influence on students' behavior in a school. The Post Conference invites adults in the school to take ownership (even in part) for behaviors that resulted in students committing harms in the school or classroom community.

Because this model of tier-one, whole-school climate management suggests that adults (collectively) take ownership for behaviors in classrooms and schools, Restorative Justice Post Conferences can be hastily seen by teachers as personal attacks on them instead of opportunities for personal reflection. This happened in a case with a student named Jobe and a Post Conference with his teacher Ms. Jefferson. Many teachers in our school knew Jobe, not because he frequently got into trouble (which he did) but mostly because he was an extremely likable kid. He was funny, handsome, and well-mannered. He always said good morning to adults on campus with a genuine smile and an upbeat voice. He was a very easy kid to like.

Jobe had a run-in with his teacher Ms. Jefferson. Jobe was a student with special needs. His classroom assignment was a self-contained class, meaning that Jobe spent most of his instructional day in Ms. Jefferson's class. The issue that Jobe had was he wanted to leave class early to use the restroom moments before a bell to change classes was going to ring, which was against school rules. Jobe was insistent. But Ms. Jefferson wasn't having it. Jobe had been referred to administrators multiple times for disciplinary infractions, so another infraction was sure to result in an out-of-school consequence for Jobe. One minute before the bell to change classes was scheduled to ring, Jobe walked out of class without permission. Ms. Jefferson was incensed. Jobe had defied her direction, undermined her authority, and challenged her control of her classroom. She referred Jobe to an administrator for insubordination.

Instead of suspending Jobe, the administrator referred Jobe to the Restorative Justice Tribunal. In the Tribunal, Jobe said Ms. Jefferson was yelling at him. He didn't like Ms. Jefferson yelling at him in front of his peers, and that's why he walked out of class. Jobe knew he shouldn't have walked out of class and willingly wrote Ms. Jefferson an apology letter.

When it was time to read the apology letter to Ms. Jefferson, Jobe had to get himself 'psyched up' to do it. Jobe had severe learning disabilities and sometimes experienced anxiety before moments he perceived as stressful. Coach Esaw helped Jobe get his mind right, and they walked into Ms. Jefferson's classroom together.

When they got to Ms. Jefferson's class, Jobe accidentally knocked over a soda that was sitting on Ms. Jefferson's desk. Soda spilled everywhere. It got all over everything on Ms. Jefferson's desk: the books, papers, pens, everything. The soda spill happened right as Jobe began to read his apology letter. That triggered something in Ms. Jefferson, and she became 'beet red' mad. She started yelling at Jobe,

"What are you doing! I told you that you have to be more careful!"

Coach Esaw saw what was happening and in a calm voice said to Ms. Jefferson, "It's okay, Ms. Jefferson. Accidents happen. Do you want us to come back another time?"

Those words in Ms. Jefferson's ear seemed to bring her back to the moment they were all sharing. She took a breath. She became calm.

"No. It's fine. It's totally okay."

Jobe then helped Ms. Jefferson clean-up the spilled soda. Jobe read his apology letter. Ms. Jefferson accepted Jobe's apology. Then, Jobe and Coach Esaw left.

That incident apparently weighed on Ms. Jefferson because she brought it up in her Post Conference about the incident with Ms. Green. Ms. Jefferson told Ms. Green that for days she had been reflecting on why she chose to teach students with severe learning disabilities. She said she reconnected with her purpose for teaching.

As we say while gambling in Las Vegas, here's the kicker. Ms. Jefferson then apologized to Ms. Green for something she said to Ms. Green several years prior. Years before this conversation, Ms. Jefferson told Ms. Green that students in the Severe Learning Disabilities program could not learn. Perhaps it was seeing that Jobe was capable of writing a well-written, heartfelt apology letter. Perhaps it was seeing that Jobe was capable of contrition and eloquently expressing why he should not have walked out of class. Perhaps she felt ashamed when she saw Coach Esaw show Jobe so much patience and care while she showed so little. Whatever the reason, Ms. Jefferson told Ms. Green that her incident with Jobe and reflections in the

Restorative Justice Post Conference made her rethink her belief in her students and their ability to learn.

It's true that for every single Tribunal that convenes, some harm has been committed by a student. Still, we cannot ignore that adults are the most influential force in establishing culture, expectations, and behavior boundaries in a school or classroom. Adults have an extraordinary influence on how students choose to behave in schools. When students know how caring adults expect them to behave, that knowledge impacts students' decision-making.

During a Restorative Justice Post Conference, the Facilitators meet with the referring teacher. An administrator, someone other than the person who refers students to the Restorative Justice Tribunal, also attends the Post Conference. Together they review the referral, and then a Facilitator asks the teacher the same questions Facilitators ask students at the Tribunal:

- ◆ What happened?
- ◆ What were the effects of what happened on you as a teacher and how did those actions affect others?
- ◆ What is your (the teacher's) responsibility in that specific situation to help make the classroom community better?
- ◆ What's the solution?

Post Conferences with teachers are nothing short of illuminating. In these meetings, we often find that the root of conflicts between students and teachers are misunderstandings that can be cleared up with better communication between them. I want to say the establishment of a better relationship between students and teachers would resolve many of these challenges, but that would be an oversimplification. Positive relationships between students and teachers are important; however, the net positive impact of relationships can be diminished when structures and processes to help classroom communication and to help teachers and students 'do school' during stressful circumstances are missing.

Some people who are great at establishing relationships still have difficulty with processes they use to communicate, particularly when someone in the relationship is having personal/ emotional difficulty or experiencing personal trauma. While positive relationships are essential, having a process to communicate effectively is even more critical. It may be possible to resolve some behavior conflicts between students and teachers, even when they may not have the best relationship with each other, if clear communication processes exist. Feeling able to communicate with someone lights a pathway to establishing a relationship. However, a relationship is not absolutely necessary to communicate with someone and learn what they need in a moment. Being open to 'hearing' what a student needs in a key moment could prevent a negative behavioral interaction in a classroom.

During Post Conferences, a Facilitator will share some of the back story that surfaced during the Restorative Justice Tribunal to outline the behavioral interaction from the student's perspective. This often includes sharing circumstances that influenced the student's in-class behavior. A student's family member may have been sick the night before a behavior incident, resulting in the student feeling anxious in class. The student may have worked until after midnight and had to wake up at 5:30 the morning of an incident to take their siblings to elementary school, causing them to be tired and grouchy in class. Perhaps the student who said she was speaking Spanish to her peer really was asking her peer an academic question and not saying anything inappropriate. The way the teacher redirected the student for talking in Spanish may have been—just as the student said—unnecessarily confrontational, publicly humiliating, and unnecessarily elevated into a power struggle.

These are the kinds of anecdotes that surface during Restorative Justice Post Conferences, and administrators get an opportunity to listen and identify which teachers need a different level of administrative support. Post Conferences are not the time for an administrator to give advice or direction to teachers, because the Post Conferences must be a safe space for teachers to be reflective. This means that administrators can't call teachers into their office and give them directions based on what they learn in Restorative Justice Post Conferences. Administrators rarely speak during Post Conferences. These meetings must remain safe spaces for all involved.

I remember when we launched the Restorative Justice Tribunal and started facilitating Post Conferences; two problems emerged. The first problem was that the administrator I assigned to supervise restorative justice did not consistently accompany Restorative Justice Facilitators to Post Conferences as I directed. My rationale for having the administrator attend the conference was to ensure Restorative Justice Facilitators never had to navigate a situation in which a teacher became mean or disrespectful during the Post Conference protocol. Different people have different perspectives on how classroom and schoolwide discipline should look. If a teacher is predisposed to punishment instead of restorative practices, the Post Conference discussion could get dicey. I wanted no Restorative Justice Facilitator to ever have to experience verbal abuse or disrespect from any of their peers.

The second problem that surfaced was, as I shared earlier, some teachers blew off the Post Conferences. That's when I had to intervene by emailing them to affirm my expectation that teachers with scheduled Restorative Justice Post Conferences attend them. These meetings were purposefully scheduled far enough in advance to respect teachers' schedules and other teaching responsibilities. Also, the conferences usually lasted no longer than 15 minutes. If a teacher missed a Post Conference more than once, the meeting was rescheduled to happen in my office with my participation. However, to date, that step has not been necessary.

The Post Conference affords adults structured reflection time to explore ways they could have approached a situation differently and/or reevaluate structures that may be contributing to students making poor behavioral choices. Because administrators participate in the Tribunal Post Conferences with teachers, sometimes it is the administrator who has to do some self-reflection. This is because the administrator also must do his or her part to create classroom conditions that are conducive for learning. I don't believe that harms can be repaired in a restorative justice system without opportunities for all parties involved to reflect and process their behaviors in a situation. When done well, Restorative Justice Post Conferences evolve into effective, non-threatening professional development tools that help adults in a school develop behavior management strategies and higher degrees of empathy for students.

Tribunals Repair Fractured Classroom Relationships

Restorative Justice began in the court system, and offenders are highly motivated to be reflective when one's freedom hangs in the balance. Also, when someone suffers a harm, often a significant harm, because of an offender's behavior in a court-based restorative justice system, the victim is also compelled to reflect—if only because of the emotions triggered by the harm that was done. In the court system, particularly in the juvenile justice system, a judge can assign a juvenile offender to mandatory counseling. At a minimum, judges assign juvenile offenders probation officers upon their release, and those probation officers function often in the role of therapists, helping offenders process their daily interactions and reflect on the harms they have caused to others. The court system can also provide victims with referrals to groups to help victims talk through the emotions they experience as the result of a harm that has occurred.

In traditional disciplinary structures in schools, none of these supports exist. Students get suspended. They get sent home. They return to school. They return to the same classes and interact with the same teachers and students they may have had conflicts with before they got suspended. There is no structured reflection of the school's code of discipline for the student offender. There is no structured reflection or counseling for the student or teacher who experienced a harm by the offender's actions.

The last thing we want to do in schools after a student is suspended is send them back into a classroom where the relationship between them and the teacher remains fractured. The Restorative Justice Post Conference helps to close this gap, facilitating the reflection required to ensure bridges can be reestablished. This ensures classroom environments are welcoming to students after they return to class after harming the classroom community.

11

Supervision and Ongoing Support

The Restorative Justice Biweekly Meeting

What gets checked on gets done. To ensure your Restorative Justice Tribunal and overall restorative justice program succeeds, check on it to make sure it runs properly. I thought I had done an adequate job of setting the program up for success when I first launched the Restorative Justice Tribunal in my school. All of the people involved with the roll out were part of the planning conversations. All of the people involved went with me to a Restorative Justice Conference. I didn't exactly plan it this way, but all of the people involved in the roll out were African-American staff, so I, inadvertently, increased the likelihood of staff members' investment in the program's success—since the problem was the disproportionate suspension of Black students. At least I thought I did. All of the proverbial checkboxes were checked for a successful rollout. However, things didn't quite go that way.

When we launched the Restorative Justice Tribunal, the team started to hear cases. However, they only heard three or four cases a week. The problem with that was the Deans' Office received upwards of 60 behavioral referrals a day. I put Assistant Principal Sams in charge of supervising the restorative justice program. She was charming and beloved by the school community. I liked her a lot as her personality was magnetic. She had incredible potential as a leader. However, she wasn't the most efficient administrator. When her work got done, it got done slowly, which wasn't a great fit for a busy school. I would check in with Ms. Sams about the program and get similar responses, "Everything is fine" and "The team is ironing out the wrinkles." She assured me the small number of cases the restorative justice team was hearing would pick up soon. To me, this made sense because we were just getting restorative justice started. I had an idea, but I didn't know how it would operationalize. In the grand scheme of things, four students a week was four more students we took off the path to being referred to an alternative school for receiving multiple suspensions in a school year. Then, two or three weeks of hearing four cases a week turned into two months. I was no longer was okay with 'ironing out the wrinkles' being the reason the restorative justice team was hearing so few cases.

Return on investment weighed heavily on my mind. I had asked the big boss for a full position to implement my ideas for a restorative justice program. I had to demonstrate a better return on the district's investment of money. I promised the big boss we would demonstrate a solution to reduce disproportionate suspension and expulsion that we could 'scale up' and replicate in other schools, and in the unlikely event that our effort failed, we would learn significant lessons that would help the district move forward in its goal to reduce suspensions and expulsions of African-American students. It did not appear we were on a pathway to success. What was troubling me more than potentially failing to demonstrate a return on investment was that the math didn't make sense.

Four cases a week? The year we launched the Restorative Justice Tribunal at my school, while students' behavior was better than it had been in the years before we started the program, their behavior was still 'off the hook.' There were still students who were defiant to their teachers. There were still students who were disruptive in class. There were so many behavior referrals from staff that the Tribunal could've heard four cases every morning, rather than four cases every week. Things weren't adding up. Right around that time, Ms. Green came into my office one day, asked if I had a moment to talk privately, and she closed the door. She voiced her concerns.

"She's not helping us. She's not listening to us."

"What do you mean?" I asked.

"We keep telling her that teachers aren't releasing the students. We keep saying the Deans' Office isn't sending cases. We keep telling Ms. Sams. Sams isn't listening to us."

Ms. Green confirmed my suspicions. I wasn't surprised, but I was disappointed. When I first asked Ms. Green to be the anchor of my school's restorative justice program, she did not want to do it. My request angered her. Ms. Green was a school counselor deeply committed to her caseload of students. She wanted no part of anything that would take her away from her counseling duties. Now, Ms. Green was in my office, a full believer in the power of the Restorative Justice Tribunal. She was done with allowing her immediate supervisor to undermine the program's ability to help children and their families. She confirmed what I suspected. There was a barrier to progress that I needed to remove. That was all I needed to hear. That was the day I took over the supervision of restorative justice. That was the day I mandated biweekly meetings to hold administrators accountable for their roles in making the restorative justice program work.

The First Restorative Justice Team Meeting

I asked my secretary (who is amazing by the way) to schedule the first restorative justice administrative meeting, and I wanted everyone with any role in the program there. I directed the assistant principal who supervised the program to be there, the deans who referred students to the Restorative Justice Tribunal, and the three Tribunal Facilitators. While everyone maintained professional decorum, I implored everyone at the team meeting to speak frankly and candidly. In my mind, the district depended on us to find a solution to disproportionate suspensions and expulsions. They'd given us money they didn't have to get us to figure it out, so we were going to do just that.

More importantly, we owed it to the scores of students in the district being hit with 'ticky-tack' suspensions to figure out a solution. I needed everyone at the meeting to speak freely and not censor their thinking. I needed everyone on the team to feel empowered to be creative problem-solvers if we were to make the program work. The most challenging thing I had to do was create a space where licensed personnel could safely critique the effectiveness of the program components, which included implicitly critiquing the performance and decision-making of administrators. Some of the administrators on that inaugural team most certainly did not like having their power or authority challenged by licensed personnel. Two of the administrators were new, and it was in their nature to project power—particularly when anyone questioned their authority. By this point, though, the Restorative Justice Facilitators were so frustrated by how the restorative justice program was going that they could care less about upsetting the administrators' sensibilities. It helped that the Facilitators were as courageous as they were passionate about restorative practices. Ms. Green, in particular, was especially prepared to speak up about the challenges she experienced getting the Restorative Justice Tribunal workflow in place. She was done with Ms. Sams.

That first meeting was tense. It ran differently than other meetings I facilitated up until that point. It was strikingly different. I'm certain the heaviness in the room made everyone feel like somebody was 'in trouble' or somebody messed up. It was crystal clear to the team that I had gathered them together to get information because the restorative justice program was sputtering. The program was hobbling along instead of running smoothly. The number of cases was so triflingly low. Everyone knew we had to get the restorative justice program on track.

It didn't take long for answers to emerge. I found that the deans did not clearly understand what information to send to

Facilitators for every Restorative Justice Tribunal. When packets of information for cases were sent to the Tribunal Facilitators, essential information was missing. The Deans' Office had a tough time getting permission slips back from students. The way the deans or the deans' secretary described the restorative justice program to students or their families was inconsistent, if she described the program at all. Teachers were not sending students to the Tribunals. And most concerning to me was that teachers were not showing up for their Restorative Justice Post Conferences to discuss incidents with the Facilitators. So much was not happening, and it all came out at that meeting. Ms. Sams outranked, in terms of organizational structure, all of the employees who were essential to making the Tribunal work, and the process wasn't working. It was clear that Ms. Sams, the charismatic and beloved administrator I put in charge of supervising the restorative justice program, was asleep at the wheel.

While it wasn't in the front of my mind, I had another motivation for making sure restorative justice worked at my school. Failures by African-American administrators in my district were rarely treated as just simple failures. Failures by Black school leaders were used as indictments of the competence of current, future, and past Black school leaders, and I refused to contribute negatively to that narrative.

After that first RJ biweekly meeting, the workflow for the restorative justice program got on track. The messaging about the Restorative Justice Tribunal became more consistent. We became more efficient at getting permission from parents for their students to participate. Three or four cases in a week increased to ten or fifteen. Then, the number of cases jumped to 15 or 20 a week. For a while in that first year, we ran Restorative Justice Tribunals in two locations simultaneously. The Deans' Office was getting cases to the Facilitators more efficiently. Case folders were complete before they were sent to the Tribunal. I had an executive coach working with me that year. I asked her to plug into restorative justice to hedge against the difficulties I had with Ms. Sams, and her intervention and assistance were amazing. Post Conferences with teachers were happening. We were rolling. We were learning a lot and keeping many students off the track to suspensions and expulsions.

How the Restorative Justice Biweekly Meetings Evolved

The team met again two weeks later. The meeting had an entirely different tone this time. We felt good about our work because we could see our progress. There we were sitting at the long table in the Principal's Conference Room. Ms. Green was ready to go with the agenda for the meeting. I like to empower teacher leaders to lead, so I delegated the creation of the agenda and the meeting facilitation to Ms. Green. While I developed the meeting structure, the biweekly meetings worked because the people closest to the work took ownership of meeting facilitation and agenda-setting. Ms. Green and I met between meetings, and she pitched potential agenda items. She did an excellent job of identifying the topics that merited whole-team discussion.

The first agenda item for the restorative justice biweekly meetings was always the same, reviewing case data. We discussed the number of Restorative Justice Tribunals and Restorative Justice Circles that were held since the last meeting. We also looked at the total number of Tribunals and Circles that had occurred up until that point in the school year. As the years progressed, we added another data point to the agenda. We wanted to know the number of restorative justice cases that had been heard in a school year compared to the number of cases heard in the previous school year. This data point served as a sort of productivity/quality control.

If the number of cases at one point in a school year was lower than the number of cases the previous year, we investigated more closely. We looked closely to see if there was a workflow problem to prevent the team from erroneously concluding that fewer students were being referred for fewer infractions. The next agenda items were a combination of workflow issues that surfaced that needed to be resolved or a review of anything unusual that surfaced during a case or Post Conference that merited team discussion. For instance, one time after

Ms. Green and Coach Esaw were asked to implement the program districtwide, a new employee began to run Restorative Justice Tribunals. Instead of running Tribunals for 15 minutes like she was trained to do, she allowed Tribunals to run for up to 30 minutes. This kept students (offenders and Peer Advocates) out of class for extended periods of time, unnecessarily. That became a discussion point at a biweekly team meeting.

In another instance, a new assistant principal responsible for discipline referred an unsuitable case to restorative justice. A student had said something in class that was not blatantly sexually offensive to others but had a sexually suggestive undertone. There is no way on earth that case should have been referred to the Tribunal where Peer Advocates could be exposed to the sexually suggestive content of the case, but a rookie administrator referred it. This is another reason why, in our protocols, we have an experienced or senior administrator present for most of the time that Tribunal cases are heard to provide oversight to the Facilitators. When I train Restorative Justice Facilitators in my own school and across the nation, I repeatedly say that if anything starts to go wrong in a case, stop the Tribunal immediately. Refer the case back to the administrator who referred it and proceed with the discipline the student would have received if they were not referred to the Tribunal.

That second meeting, like all the restorative justice meetings, ended with the same question, "What can we do to make the program better?" The responses this question gets are illuminating. Because it is the last question, admittedly, sometimes meeting participants are too tired to respond. Other times, the question sparks extraordinarily creative thinking. The need to make wraparound services more robust in our restorative justice program began as an answer to this question. For instance, I am currently working with community allies to provide my students and staff access to licensed therapists at no charge to most families. We also increased our engagement with various community agencies to provide families with access to social services because we saw how difficulties that impacted families made it hard for some students to learn and stay focused in school. Actively searching for ways to make the restorative justice program better keeps the group focused on continuous improvement as a goal in and of itself. It drives us to identify innovations that will benefit the entire school community.

I think it is noteworthy to discuss the location where we held our Restorative Justice Tribunal biweekly team meetings—the Principal's Conference Room. The Principal's Conference Room in my school is a public space. There is a staff refrigerator in there. There is also a microwave oven and a water cooler in this room. It was common for staff members to walk into the meeting to fill up their water bottles while we were meeting. The content of biweekly meetings wasn't a secret, nor was it a situation where we would invite staff members to pull up a chair to participate in the meetings. I cannot say we planned things this way. It just happened.

Those restorative justice biweekly meetings in that public space were a symbol of our belief system as a school and my philosophy as a principal. Faculty and staff were able to see our commitment to using alternatives to punishment to change students' behavior. I believe our visible commitment to finding alternatives other than punishment to influence students' behavior also prompted faculty and staff to reevaluate their own perspectives on punishment as a classroom management tool. The public nature of our biweekly meetings announced that we were dedicated to improving classroom management and reducing the suspension and expulsion rates of students.

12

Tribunals Are a Solution for Diverse Students

The Restorative Justice Tribunal has always been committed to adapting to the needs of students. So, it is important to share how students influence me to modify our approach to restorative justice. In one instance, students convinced me to include behavior infractions in our restorative response plan that I was, initially, philosophically opposed to including.

Wisdom Out of the Mouths of Children

To remain attuned to the needs of students, I started something called 'Lunch and Listen.' It is an opportunity for students to have lunch with me—my treat—and share their experiences, thoughts, and opinions about the school directly with the principal. The only thing I ask of participants is if they are having difficulty with an adult on campus, to refrain from identifying the adult by name. I also ask that they do not say things to make it easy for participants to figure out the teacher with whom they're having a problem. Without question, I would address their concerns, but under no circumstances would I support speaking ill of community members in a public forum.

One day, six students and I were together for lunch in the Principal's Conference Room for a 'Lunch and Listen' session. There were four young ladies and two gentlemen. The students happened to be juniors and seniors. Most of them were involved in clubs and organizations on campus. The group was comprised of Hispanic, African-American, and Caucasian students. The group was a nice representation of the student body.

We had finished our Chinese food, which is what they wanted. They had finished sharing what they liked about the school and what they wanted me to ensure continued happening at Cheyenne. We had moved on in our discussion to their areas of concern. A student named Kendra was at the 'Lunch and Listen' that day. Kendra had some troubles early in her high school experience, but she was finding her way behaviorally and academically. She had participated in our Restorative Justice Tribunal, formed some opinions of the process, and she was not happy with me. When the conversation provided the window of opportunity she needed, she looked at me with steely eyes. She said, "Dr. Robbins, I heard you won't let students who fight go through restorative justice." She left it right there, hanging in the air—daring me not to address her concern directly. And when I looked at the other students, some of them had similar looks on their faces. With perfect timing for the moment, one folded her arms across her chest, tilted her head to the side, looked at me over her glasses, and popped a bubble gum bubble. It was a setup! And I could not have been more proud of them for advocating for themselves and their peers.

I explained my position that the restorative justice program was designed to divert students with low-level infractions from out-of-school consequences. The theoretical plan of action for our restorative justice program was to focus on students who committed low-level infractions. There were enough behavioral challenges to address. The volume of students committing low-level infractions was metastasizing into overwhelming, unnecessarily high numbers of out-of-school consequences for students. So many students were receiving out-of-school consequences for minor infractions, such as refusing to sit in their correct seats or talking back to a teacher, that I did not want to ask the

Restorative Justice Tribunal Facilitators to add anything else to their already overflowing plates. I was not okay with low-level infractions putting students on the pathway to suspension, so that's what I wanted to focus on with our restorative practices, not major infractions like fighting.

Kendra wasn't accepting my explanation nor was her girl-friend, who was blowing bubble gum bubbles with her head cocked to the side. Kendra would not be moved. She calmly retorted, "Dr. Robbins, people are getting in fights and coming back to school without working out the stuff they fought over in the first place. Either you help them work it out or social media will help them work it out. I think you know which would be best." After that, the other students piled on. Eventually, I threw my hands up in submission, and they all laughed. I couldn't deny it. They were right.

That night I figured out how to integrate the students' rec-ommendations into our restorative justice program. I took their recommendations to the next restorative justice biweekly plan-ning meeting, and we fine-tuned how to implement a restorative justice solution for students who fought on campus. The solution we initiated will be discussed further in a later chapter.

Tribunals and Students With Special Needs

When we first launched the Restorative Justice Tribunal, I speci-fied that the program must serve all students. Therefore, we made a conscious effort to ensure the program worked for stu-dents with special needs. The key difference in the Tribunal when the offender is a student with special needs is the extra steps Facilitators take to address their specialized educational requirements. This is especially important for students with severe emotional disabilities who attend most of their classes in self-contained classrooms.

For these students, besides their behavioral referral, witness statements, and other relevant case documents, we also send Tribunal Facilitators a copy of their Individual Education Plan (IEP) and Behavioral Intervention Plan, if they have one.

Depending on the student and the infraction, the administrator may also ask a special education professional, such as a case manager or behavior interventionist, to sit with the student when they attend their Restorative Justice Tribunal.

One of the primary purposes of an Individualized Education Plan is to ensure that students with disabilities have their educational needs met and can access the general education curriculum. We want to ensure that students with special needs can access the socioemotional curriculum in the restorative justice program as well as the Tribunal's structures, processes, and functions.

It is prudent sometimes to ask a staff member from the Special Education Department to assist with this. We have done this in our own restorative justice programming and have had enormous success. After the offender proposes a solution to repair the harm their behavior caused, it is my recommendation that the special education professional accompanies the Facilitator and student to another room to help them process the events of the Tribunal while the Tribunal panel deliberates.

13

Can Circles and Tribunals Coexist?

Circles? In an Off-the-Hook Classroom?

Before we get into a discussion about Circles, I'd like you to
indulge me for a moment.

Imagine the least effective manager of classroom culture and
climate you can think of. I'll paint a picture for readers who
have never worked in a school. Mr. Straights is a highly skilled
teacher with deep knowledge of content standards. However,
he has difficulty managing his classroom. It is common for
Mr. Straights to bring his class to attention, and moments later,
his students would begin having side conversations while he
was talking. Mr. Straights would then scream at students to 'get
them under control.' Feeling disrespected, the students would
scream back at him. Mr. Straights referred at least 15 students
a day to his school administrators for not following his classroom
directives. His students would not sit in their assigned seats.
They talked at inappropriate times. His students said inappropriate things. Mr. Straights' yearly appraisals consistently
reflected his poor classroom management, and his overall

appraisals suffered because his lack of classroom management negatively affected his teaching effectiveness.

There may be multiple Mr. Straights in a school, depending on the size of the school. There may be five Mr. Straights in an elementary school. There may be ten Mr. Straights in a secondary school. There may be more. And those teachers can impact the lives of so many children.

Now imagine those teachers with poor classroom management stopping instruction to bring a class together to run a Restorative Justice Circle.

Can you see those Circles going well? Perhaps after one or two hours of professional development, do you see those teachers running Circles that go well? What if one of those teachers has particularly disruptive students in class? How do you see those Circles going?

Now, imagine one more thing for me.

This time, imagine the most effective teacher in a school with a class of students who are far below academic standards, and that teacher's goal is to get those students as close as possible to performing on grade level. Perhaps there is a standardized assessment on which the school wants those students to show academic growth or proficiency? For high poverty schools, this problem isn't imaginary or rhetorical. It is real. Widespread racial segregation in schools has driven substantial gaps in academic achievement between African-American and Hispanic students and their Caucasian peers (Meckler, 2019). While every teacher may not be 'highly effective' as defined by a district's appraisal system, the need to accelerate achievement and close achievement gaps is more common. The National Assessment of Educational Progress scores in Reading echoes this urgency as fourth and eighth grade 2019 reading scores decreased compared to 2017 results (Hussar et al., 2020). The Coronavirus pandemic will likely exacerbate this problem as involuntary homeschooling cannot replace face-to-face instruction for students who need academic acceleration and supports. As a result of the pandemic, African-American and Latino students will lose nine or ten months of learning before they start the 2020–2021 school year

(Goldstein, 2020). Who knows how much learning will be lost during the school year as school districts find balance between safe instruction in the midst of Covid-19 and effective instruction for all students and staff? Multiply that effective teacher by five if you work in an elementary school. That's five elementary teachers on a staff serving, at least, 60 students. Multiply that effective teacher by ten if you work in a secondary school. Those ten teachers most likely work with upwards of 250 students that perform below grade-level standards.

Now, imagine those teachers periodically stopping instruction to run Restorative Justice Circles to repair harms to students in classes. What if there are several harms in a day or several harms in a class period? What if those teachers have particularly challenging students in their classes? How much lost instructional time is reasonable in the interest of using classroom-based Restorative Justice Circles to establish a positive classroom climate?

Many students enter my school three or four grade levels behind in reading and/or math proficiency. The school-based restorative justice model I decided to implement couldn't sacrifice class time, not even to divert students from out-of-school consequences. The need to improve achievement and divert students from out-of-school consequences were equally important. While I would like to believe the public would appreciate dramatically reduced suspension and expulsion rates over everything else, I suspect that success at reducing suspensions and expulsions would be eclipsed by a failure to make identifiable, quantifiable academic progress.

This is why in the school-based model this book proposes— Restorative Justice Circles—is used, but not in a way that regularly interrupts classroom instruction. The times when we felt compelled to facilitate a whole-class Circle was when harms occurred that affected entire classes—to the point the harm derailed entire classes from focusing on learning. For example, one classroom community was upset and could not move past an incident where one of their peers used a gender-identity slur toward a student in their class. The teacher addressed the behavior, but many students could not excuse or move past that the offender in this case was so mean and hurtful to their classmate. Classroom instruction was so sidetracked that we had to facilitate a whole-class Restorative Justice Circle to repair the harm done in that class community. Then, we could refocus the class on instruction and repair the damage done to the relationships among peers. Ms. Green facilitated the Circle, and it was wildly successful.

Who Should Run Restorative Circles in Schools?

I believe Circles succeed in my school because the Restorative Justice Facilitators—in their areas of expertise and licensure—are trained to facilitate challenging conversations. Further professional development in restorative justice techniques enhanced training they already had. It takes specific skills to run Restorative Justice Circles well. These skills are essential when cases are sophisticated and when students' out-of-school needs significantly impact their academic performance and progress.

Schools should ensure a school counselor is on their restorative justice team. School counselors are trained to help students cope with the circumstances and stressors that interfere with learning. I believe the skills required to facilitate Restorative Justice Circles well are anchored in the fundamentals of group counseling. School counselors and school social workers, along with school psychologists, are the professionals in schools with the most training at facilitating group counseling. That being said, I do think many elementary schools' Restorative Circles can be facilitated with staff members other than the school counselors, school psychologists, or social workers—provided the harms elementary school offenders commit aren't incredibly voluminous or sophisticated and the elementary students are not experiencing issues outside of school that require counseling services or therapeutic supports.

Unfortunately, the ratio of counselors to students in many schools and districts is not ideal. School psychologists are so busy performing evaluations for special education cases and responding to students in crises that they have limited time to provide preventative therapeutic services to students. It is my hope that through the Restorative Justice Tribunal, more school psychologists, social workers, and school counselors will increase opportunities to provide preventative therapeutic supports to students and help them resolve conflicts with each other and/ or within themselves.

How Restorative Circles Coexist With Tribunals

Let me be more specific about how Restorative Circles coexist with the Restorative Justice Tribunal. We used Circles to serve an urgent need. We initially used Circles as our restorative response to verbal altercations among students.

Verbal altercations mostly happened during lunch periods, followed by after school, and least frequently between classes during hallway passing periods. Verbal altercations tended to be extremely public, and students felt an overwhelming peer pressure to 'save face' during verbal altercations. Therefore, the arguments were often catalysts for brawls between multiple students. The incubation period between verbal altercations and the moment that students fought (if the verbal altercation progressed that far) created a tension on campus that was thick and palpable. Verbal conflicts between factions of students became 'hood news' that got amplified by verbal altercation participants, their friends, and by virtual bystanders on various social media platforms.

Some of the students who got into these verbal altercations were gang-affiliated, and that skyrocketed the danger of these altercations. When particularly aggressive verbal confrontations occurred, I used to say to administrators, "Find *every* kid involved. Call their parents. And get them off campus before lunch!" If we couldn't find all the students involved before lunch, things often got ugly. The minutes of administrative lunch duty felt like days. Restorative Justice Circles were the key to relieving the tension these verbal altercations caused. Circles kept kids safe after verbal altercations erupted because we could get students together to clear up misunderstandings and squash any beef between them.

Because Restorative Justice Circles were high stakes and had implications for students' safety, I was thankful that Ms. Green and Coach Esaw were on staff to facilitate them. Both had 'street credibility' with our students, the training to facilitate therapeutic talk with students, and they were able to help students resolve many conflicts before they erupted into violence.

Restorative Circles After Students Threw Hands

The other way we used Circles was to relieve any lingering tensions that may exist between students who got suspended for fighting—before they returned to school. You have to understand, and I can't say it enough. I had no intention of assigning a restorative response to students who fought on campus. It was only after steady pressure from students and their sensible arguments that I acquiesced to their requests.

Students knew that if their peers who got suspended for fighting decided to fight on campus again, and that fight was bad enough, their friends would most likely be arrested by school police, charged, and introduced (or maybe pushed deeper) into the juvenile justice system. The students wanted me to stop that from happening and do all I could to stop that. I wanted the same. My students saw Restorative Justice Circles as a solution to this problem.

Initially, I resisted. I was convinced my restorative justice team didn't have enough personnel to do what the students were asking. After all, our restorative justice program was designed to address low-level offenses. Admittedly, I was stuck on that founding principle.

I didn't ignore the students, though. I did raise their concerns in our restorative justice biweekly meetings as they asked. In fact, I raised their concerns multiple times, vetting the possibility of including fighting as an infraction that would result in some sort of restorative response. I had to be persuasive because the restorative justice team was against the idea, same as I was when I first considered it. Initially, the restorative justice team decided that:

1. Fighting was not a low-level offense.
2. Unless it was a case of battery (which also wasn't a low-level offense), there wasn't a victim whose harm required repairing.
3. Saying that the community was harmed by the fighters was not a strong enough argument when you weighed the fact that the program was designed to divert students who committed low-level offenses from the pathway of suspension and expulsion.

Therefore, we kept fighting on the regular disciplinary response track.

But I came around to the students' side of the argument. They changed my mind, and I felt they were right. We *did* need some sort of restorative response before students who fought could return to campus. When students on my campus got into fights, they would be suspended. Then, days later, the students who fought would return to campus without receiving any school-based intervention to address whatever it was that caused them to fight. The same heaviness that existed after verbal altercations existed in the school after fights, especially when the students who fought returned to campus after serving their out-of-school consequences. As the principal teacher in the building, I had done nothing about it. At the beginning of our sixth year of running restorative justice, I told the team we were including fighting as an infraction that would result in a restorative response. It was no longer a choice. It was happening.

So much could go wrong in our restorative justice program that year. I had three new administrators to train to administer restorative justice and to run the program. Ms. Green and Coach Esaw had just been promoted to train the entire school district on restorative practices, so they were splitting their workday between my school and being in the field to train teachers and leaders throughout the district. The year that Ms. Green and Coach Esaw were promoted, behavior issues were escalating in the building, in proportion with an escalation of gang activity in the neighborhood and city. We added this new pathway for a restorative response in spite of all these factors.

Here is what happened the first time we convened a Circle after a fight.

A group of young ladies had been feuding over conflicts they had with each other since middle school (you can't make this stuff up). Things boiled over one day on campus, and they got into a fight. After an out-of-school consequence, we sent permission slips home to ask their parents for permission to bring the ladies together into a Restorative Justice Circle. All but one parent agreed. The school counselor and the school social worker (our Facilitators) ran the Circle. The experience was breathtakingly amazing.

My school has one of the highest populations of African-American students in the district. At one point during the Circle, one of the participants said to Ms. Green, "We're all sisters. We should be building each other up, not tearing each other down."

I've been a believer ever since.

The Circle experience allows us to teach social and emotional lessons right there on the spot. The Facilitators helped the young ladies learn strategies to be reflective and to navigate the emotions they were feeling that prompted them to fight each other. This is just one example of the power of the Restorative Justice Circles.

References

Goldstein, D. (2020, June 10). *Research shows students falling months behind during virus disruptions*. Retrieved from www.nytimes.com/2020/06/05/us/coronavirus-education-lost-learning.html

Hussar, B., Zhang, J., Hein, S., Wang, K., Roberts, A., Cui, J., . . . Dilig, R. (2020). *The condition of education 2020*. NCES 2020-144. National Center for Education Statistics.

Meckler, L. (2019, September 19). *Achievement gaps in schools driven by poverty, study finds*. Retrieved from www.washingtonpost.com/local/education/achievement-gaps-in-schools-driven-by-poverty-study-finds/2019/09/22/59491778-dd73-11e9-b199-f638bf2c340f_story.html

14

Foundations for Implementation

Establish Tier-One Expectations

This book proposes a restorative approach to schoolwide behavior management. I submit, though, that other things must be in place for any behavior management approach to work in a school. If a school does not pay close enough attention to schoolwide tier-one classroom management, any restorative justice program will be overrun with referrals from teachers. There is no way around this, so attention to tier-one classroom management is essential.

Attention to tier-one classroom management requires two things. First, schools must ensure that teachers have a sense of what the overarching classroom-based tier-one expectations for students are. There must be some consensus on the basic things that everyone will expect from students and each other.

The other thing that schools must do is provide kind, but direct, administrative responses when staff members emerge who need additional support with their classroom management. These responses should provide staff members with the help they need to maintain schoolwide behavioral expectations for students.

To establish these schoolwide norms, it is critically important to bring teams of teachers together to come to a consensus.

Stay the Course for Staff Buy-In

I believe that revolution sparks counterrevolution, so it isn't advisable to ask staff members to do or address too many things at once. To ask people to do too many things (especially new things) is to set them up for failure. It is a wiser course of action to get staff members in a school to agree on the handful of things that everyone will require students to do. And when everyone doesn't honor the agreement, there must not only be an administrative response but also a peer response.

The agreement among teachers has to be a reasonable request, something so culturally appropriate to the community that teachers in the building needn't rely on a school administrator to hold their peers accountable to the expectation. The agreement must be something that teachers feel they can't live without, something that makes their job difficult if their peers don't extend professional courtesy and honor the agreement. If teachers hold this kind of stake in the agreement, they will hold themselves and each other accountable.

Admittedly, this is much easier said than done. Depending on the school, the district, and the work climate in both, collaboration can be difficult. For instance, if all is great in a district and everyone is happy, establishing and adhering to building-wide agreements is much easier. If, however, a district enters into a strike climate, the degree of difficulty to reach consensus on building-wide behavior agreements (or anything else for that matter) increases.

If a school has a student body that is compliant with their teachers, it will be easier to come to consensus about behavior expectations than it will be in a school where students chronically misbehave. In fact, in schools where students persistently challenge the authority of teachers, it is exponentially more difficult to establish, let alone maintain, behavior agreements among staff. The great American philosopher Mike Tyson once said that everyone has a plan until they get punched in the mouth. In challenging schools, where students are generally not compliant, it is important to keep this philosophical quip in mind.

Expect the emotionally draining challenges that students seem uniquely equipped to sustain for long periods. Be mindful of how formidable the will of children can be during the period dedicated to consensus-building when the team establishes their whole-school expectations. Be aware that every educator is not a gifted classroom manager. Whatever is asked of the staff, the overwhelming majority (if not everyone) must have the skills to undertake. This is true even during the points of a school year when most are fatigued or emotionally drained.

In addition to this, school administrative teams must be willing and able to validate these agreements. They must be prepared to intervene with support whenever needed. The climate of the school or district will dictate what that support looks like during times of prosperity and times of turbulence. The life cycles of most schools indicate that at some point school staff will experience both the ups and downs.

Be Clear in What Is Expected

Several factors can influence the establishment of these behavior expectations. For example, the experience level and stability of school administrative teams influence how administrative support looks for the building-wide agreements on behavior expectations. Someone assigned to a school as a substitute school principal (until a permanent leader is hired) may support building-wide behavior agreements far differently than a board-approved principal whose performance evaluation is based on the success of the school. A principal who is new to a school may support and maintain building-wide agreements for behavior expectations differently than an administrator who has been in a school for four years or more. Likewise, the school principal that has been a practicing administrator for several years may differ in approach to an administrator in the twilight of his or her career and close to retirement. Administrators at different points in their professional careers may have quite different perspectives on how to support a teacher who fails to adhere to agreements for climate and classroom management. While we may like to say that the response among these diverse leaders should not look too different, it most likely will.

Teamwork is required to develop schoolwide behavior expectations, plus the administrative and peer supportive responses when staff members deviate from those agreements. That team should not be comprised solely of administrators, nor should that team be comprised solely of the most gifted classroom managers or the most talented teachers in a school. The plan must be informed by a diversity of thoughts and opinions from several staff members, so the building-wide approach is more likely to be sustainable in the face of staff changes.

Classroom Behavior Agreements

The in-class agreements for behavior expectations in elementary schools deserve more discussion, particularly the agreements among elementary school primary grade teachers. Primary grade-level teams must be especially mindful of the agreements they establish because primary grade children are still learning how to 'do' school. This factor is critically important to keep in mind.

Agreements on classroom behaviors and procedures that are appropriate for children in kindergarten through to second grade may not be appropriate for children in third, fourth, or fifth grades. It is highly likely that the reinforcers for behavior that will open up the benefits of standards-based learning for these students will be different. Therefore, elementary classroom teachers and school leaders must be mindful of this when establishing agreements on grade-level teams, primary grades, and/or whole-school behavior expectations.

Identify Troublesome Spaces

An exercise I like to facilitate with teams of teachers and administrators is to have them identify the spaces in a school where behavior infractions happen most frequently. Then, I have them write a statement that is the 'replacement behavior' for the behavior infraction. In essence, I ask them to name the behavior they want to see in those spaces instead of the problematic behaviors they tend to see.

I require them to frame the behaviors they wish to see in positive language. For example, a behavior a school may want to see in their hallways is, "Your voice level must be respectful of the learning of others." If a school can reduce behavior infractions in the hallways, the number of referrals resulting from those spaces will reduce. It makes sense. Change the behavior in the spaces where behavior infractions occur, and the outcome is fewer referrals for that behavior and fewer that come from those spaces.

At the time of writing, my current challenge is to address negative behaviors that occur in the hallways during class periods and during the unstructured free time during lunch. Each school may have different problem areas, though many, such as hallways and stairwells, are common.

15

Final Thoughts on Derailing Jim Crow Discipline

This journey to derail Jim Crow discipline is personal for me. I would not be who I am today without the people who did not give up on me, who did not subject me to the throes of Jim Crow discipline, even when I made poor behavior choices. When I was a student at Jefferson Davis Junior High School, I was not a well-behaved student. I used to 'cut up' in classes with my neighborhood friend Dean. We were both poor students academically and very disruptive in classes.

I remember one particular day when Dean and I were being disruptive in Mr. Hester's math class. We were playing the dozens, laughing loudly, and making our peers snicker while Mr. Hester was teaching. Mr. Hester would ask us to stop talking. We would stop for a few minutes, and then we would start talking again. Mr. Hester waited out our antics and finished the 'direct instruction' part of his lesson. Then, we worked independently and practiced applying the mathematical concepts he taught to problems in our textbook.

As I reflect on this story now, I feel awful. My behavior was as ridiculous as it was uncaring for my peers' learning. I was oblivious to what the consequences could have been if Mr. Hester referred me to school administrators for behavior consequences. Mr. Hester was a patient, kind African-American man. Despite how disruptive I was, he never referred me to administrators for behavioral consequences. He called my parents. Mr. Hester assigned me detention. However, he never sent me to the Principal's Office. I believe Mr. Hester tolerated my antics because he understood the implications for any Black child, particularly for a Black boy, to be repeatedly suspended from school in Hampton, Virginia.

The community where I grew up was one where African-American people stuck together to stay safe and survive. Black children at Jefferson Davis Middle School understood unspoken rules of race outside of school, so I'm certain the adults did too. There was a community swimming pool in walking distance of my home where Black folks knew the unspoken rule that we could not swim there. There was a restaurant within walking distance of my home where we knew our parents would never take us to eat. There were areas in our city where we knew Ku Klux Klan meetings convened. I'm sure this climate of racial intolerance affected teachers. I believe Mr. Hester knew if he referred me or any of the other Black boys repeatedly for out-of-school consequences, he risked putting us on a track we may not be able to exit. Students labeled by teachers as 'difficult' were often overlooked, and little was expected of them academically. I know because little was expected of me. 'Difficult' students were promoted to their next grades poorly prepared to be successful. This is what happened to 'difficult' Black students back in the day. I don't believe it is far off the mark to what still happens to students labeled as troublemakers now.

In hindsight, I believe Mr. Hester was a saint.

I remember another moment in Mr. Hester's class that illustrates how disruptive I was in class and how uninterested I was in academics. Mr. Hester was returning math tests to our class. Dean received his test, and it was a failing grade. Mr. Hester gave me mine. It was a failing grade. I remember that failing that test would make it difficult for me to pass the quarter. Mr. Hester had our seats separated, so Dean yelled across the classroom to me, "Zac! What you get?"

I responded, "An F."

"Me too!" Dean could hardly contain his laughter. Then he said, "We should have a contest to see how many Fs we can get!"

Finding the idea hilarious, I yelled back, "Okay! Let's do it."

Absolute craziness.

This is who I was in junior high school. It remained much of who I was throughout high school until I got placed in Mr. Ponteroy's biology class in the second semester of my sophomore year. I connected with Mr. Ponteroy. Despite my reputation for being disruptive, Mr. Ponteroy believed in me. He engaged me in conversations about class content in ways that, up until that point, no teacher had. I remember one day, Mr. Ponteroy took our biology class on a walk around our high school campus to study plants. I had no interest in leaves, absolutely none. However, because Mr. Ponteroy asked me to look at leaves and plants, I was all in. Mr. Ponteroy focused on all he could find that was good in me. I liked him, so I lived up to his behavioral and academic expectations. That semester of biology changed me as I saw myself in a way I never had. I saw that I could 'do' school.

While I was not a student who was suspended often, I absolutely could have been because I was disruptive in classes. After being extended grace and having a teacher who believed in me, I stopped being so disruptive. I turned myself around behaviorally and academically. I believe that most, if not all, students can do the same. We just have to give those students love, attention, and the time they need to realize their potential. These transformations can't happen if students are suspended from school. Suspensions and expulsions unnecessarily put these epiphanies at risk. Schools must derail Jim Crow discipline. I will wrap up this book with some overarching recommendations in addition to the ones I've already shared.

School Personnel Must Be Outraged by Racial Bias

To derail Jim Crow discipline, school personnel must be outraged by racism. Caring enough to do something about racism and racial disproportionality has to evolve from 'dislike' to a 'visceral reaction,' even if that visceral reaction is internal and not easily recognizable by others. One must care enough to be incensed by how racial biases sustain disproportionate suspensions and expulsions. Simply being uncomfortable with racism, racial bias, and disproportionality is not enough to prompt people to act. Again, dislike must evolve to outrage, and the outrage can't be manufactured. It must be real. My proposal that school personnel be outraged by Jim Crow discipline is not a recommendation to fill schools with emotionally unhinged adults. On the contrary, to show outrage is to intentionally behave in ways that communicate one's belief that racial bias, racism, and resulting disproportionate outcomes are grossly offensive to decency, morality, and fairness.

You may be asking, "What should be done if people aren't outraged by racism, racial bias, and disproportionality?" My answer is, "Folks have to be taught why they should be outraged." That's what I've been doing in the narrative of this book. I know that showing outrage against Jim Crow discipline can be scary. Systems built upon the foundations of racial authority and racial exceptionalism tend to 'push back' on displays of outrage. Still, people who wish to derail Jim Crow discipline have to muster up their bravery and take comfort in the fact that they are rarely alone in their thinking. I believe there is a silent majority of decent, moral people in most schools and school districts who are outraged by racism and racial bias. The silent majority can't stand for the creation and enforcement of policies that disproportionately harm groups of people. Even if their protest is quiet, I believe honorable employees act urgently to undermine people and things that sustain new-era Jim Crow policies, laws, and decisions.

School Leaders Must Use Their Influence and Ability to Hire the Right People to Address Implicit Bias

The most significant act in public schooling is selecting a school principal. The principal has the most influence on teaching, learning, and implementing policies in a school (Allensworth, Sebring, & Hart, 2018). A primary ingredient in the recipe for a great school leader is an inability to ignore unfairness when practices create disparate outcomes. Some school leaders are naturally predisposed to be outraged by racial bias, racism, and any disproportionate outcomes resulting from the two. This is why it is important to select the right principal for a school. Principals outraged by racial bias will not allow students of color to be systematically jettisoned from school campuses. When they see this occurring, they will address it.

After selecting the school principal, the next most influential act in a school is deciding who teaches there. Staffing choices matter. There are few people in a school who can be more empowering and uplifting (or, conversely, damaging) to children than those who teach them. Principals and assistant principals outraged by racial bias are more likely to hire culturally competent faculty and staff. School superintendents, their cabinets, and the school principals they employ must deal with the problem of disproportionality. They cannot ignore that unwillingness to address racial bias contributes greatly to disproportionality. Unwillingness to address disproportionality sustains Jim Crow disciplinary practices and policies. Staff selection can remedy this. Suppose there is no outrage and no urgency to address the racial bias—in either policy or practice—at the root of disproportionate suspensions and expulsions. In that case, students of color will continue to be jettisoned out of schools at a disproportionate rate.

The Principal Is the Most Important Person in Any Effort to Derail Jim Crow Discipline

The school principal's role is essential in the effort to derail Jim Crow discipline in schools. Principals are uniquely situated to determine if disciplinary policies have a disparate impact on a particular group of students. They can empower employees to examine the implications of school policies. Moreover, the principal has the authority to launch professional development to blunt the negative effect of corrective practices.

School principals can make cultural competence a priority on a school campus. Cultural competence can mitigate against teachers' implicit biases. The training can protect against how fatigue amplifies any implicit biases teachers may have. Another thing that cultural competency training can do is help teachers work through fears they may have of losing control of their classrooms anchored in race-based cultural biases. Put another way, cultural competency training can help teachers be less fearful of not knowing how to respond when they perceive a student is 'acting Black' in some way they don't understand. Focusing on helping teachers improve their cultural competence can mitigate against this and the unnecessary labeling of students of color as troublemakers.

Principals have the most access to data related to discipline policies and practices. Schoolwide data can be analyzed to see if discipline policies have a disparate impact on students of color. It is essential to break down school data by ethnicity to ensure school policies positively impact school climate. Ethnicity data will also help facilitate positive academic outcomes for all students. The school principal is best situated to launch evidence-based interventions to address skill deficits that may underlie misbehavior. He or she should also monitor proactive efforts to diminish behavior infractions. Identifying and addressing behaviors that undermine students' ability to learn is essential in closing the loop. The principal is best situated to collect this data and determine the professional development needed to ensure school climate efforts are beneficial to all students.

Principals Must Insist That Hidden Curriculum Is Taught and Made Explicit to Students

To help more students be successful behaviorally and academically, schools must find ways to make the hidden curriculum more visible to more students. The hidden curriculum comprises unwritten, unspoken, often unintended lessons, values, and perspectives that students must master to succeed in schools. These special ways students are expected to think, talk, and behave are seldom openly discussed. Expectations embedded in the hidden curriculum can reinforce, or even contradict, the formal curriculum (Bayanfar, 2013). Students unaware of hidden curriculum rules and social norms are at a distinct disadvantage.

Teachers hold students accountable for failing to adhere to hidden curricular norms, and they sometimes punish students severely for these failures. I believe the students most vulnerable to being punished for not knowing the hidden curriculum rules are elementary school students. Suppose an elementary school teacher, especially a primary grade teacher, does a poor job teaching students social norms associated with the hidden curriculum. These students can go through school without the tools or skills they need to navigate social situations or the unspoken behavioral expectations that arise.

There is a silence about the unequal impact of school policies, which is an element in schools' hidden curriculum that must change. Schools must teach students to be resilient. This is especially true when support systems to develop resiliency are not easily available outside of school (Young, 2016).[1] Mental strength will help students navigate the hidden curriculum. The ability to communicate effectively (especially with authority figures) and self-efficacy are prerequisites to mastering hidden curriculum expectations. Schools must teach students these lessons to short-circuit the school-to-prison pipeline and derail Jim Crow discipline. When schools fail to assume responsibility for teaching these competencies to students who experience behavioral challenges, heroic teachers must become the Harriet Tubman(s); teaching students these skills to traverse the underground railroad of hidden curriculum expectations.

Schools Must Understand How Fatigue Exacerbates Implicit Biases

School leaders must remain aware of how stress and fatigue magnify how intensely employees act on their implicit biases. Researchers found that a lack of resources, an overload of demanding tasks, limited time, and other stressors create a cognitive load that contributes to activating medical practitioners' implicit biases (Burgess, Beach, & Saha, 2017). I believe stressors impact school personnel's implicit biases similarly; only the school stressors are different. When fatigue or stress strains cognition, implicit biases are more likely to influence employees' behavior and decision-making. Fatigue makes it more difficult for people to process information in the moment. Fatigue also makes people less aware of how their behavior influences their decision-making.

Some researchers believe that increasing practitioners' mindfulness will improve how they manage implicit biases. When employees are mindful, they can pay attention to their experiences in a moment, regulate their emotions, be self-aware, and have a non-judgmental orientation toward experiences (Burgess et al., 2017). Some believe mindfulness is something people get when they are born. Others reject that idea and see mindfulness as a set of skills that people can develop. In my experience, being 'mindful' about explicit biases is something practitioners can learn. School districts can facilitate employees' becoming more mindful of their implicit biases. Employees can be taught how to process and mentally role-play ways to behave in stressful situations before those situations occur.

Furthermore, teachers may better regulate their implicit biases when recognizing negative emotions that challenging situations can trigger. This strategy is akin to therapeutic role-playing. Mental health professionals have incorporated therapeutic role-playing into their counseling practices for years (Fritscher, 2019).

To Derail Jim Crow Discipline, Schools and Districts Must Not Waver in a Commitment to Implicit Bias and Diversity Training

In 2016, the United States Department of Justice called for all of its employees to receive implicit bias training ("Department of Justice Announces New Department-Wide Implicit Bias Training for Personnel," 2016). This is a shining example of the importance of institutions keeping their employees aware of how implicit biases can influence decision-making. Implicit bias training and diversity training are designed to facilitate positive group interactions, reduce prejudice, and enhance one's ability to interact with diverse people. It is often emotionally and organizationally challenging to provide diversity training to employees (Burns, Monteith, & Parker, 2017). By nature, diversity training is more personal and politically charged than other training types because—by design—diversity training challenges how people see the world and see themselves in it. The cognitive dissonance that diversity training can cause for participants can be jarring for them and their employers. Still, this training is necessary to derail Jim Crow discipline. Diversity and implicit bias training are not silver bullets. They are not an overnight remedy to unequal educational outcomes, unfair hiring practices, or employees' unfair treatment. Districts must stay the course with diversity and implicit bias training. Positive, lasting outcomes take time to develop.

Facilitate Diversity and Implicit Bias Training in Ways That Work

To be fair, there is a body of research that purports that diversity training does not work. Let me address that directly. Diversity training typically does not work when it focuses exclusively (or almost exclusively) on providing participants with examples of counterstereotypes or counternarratives of various groups. Stand-alone diversity training, where outrage against implicit bias is not woven into the fabric of an entire organizational culture, usually fails (Bezrukova, Jehn, & Spell, 2012). Diversity and implicit bias training work best when integrated as a systemic approach to behavioral and organizational change.

To make diversity and implicit bias training work, trainers should focus on multiple aspects of biases or diversity. Training that focuses on a single element—such as race—tend to be less successful. Effective diversity training also integrates various modes of instruction to reach training outcomes. This helps appeal to different learning styles. Diversity and implicit bias training that works includes a combination of lectures, video conferencing, and discussions, to name a few modes of instruction (Bezrukova et al., 2012).

Some claim that diversity training does not work or is not worth the cost in time and resources. Others will disagree with diversity or implicit bias training of any kind because they have internal prejudicial motivations (Burns et al., 2017). That is, they define themselves by their perceived superiority and intolerance of others. These people are said to have a 'bias blind spot.' That is, they can see bias in others but not themselves. For participants with a bias blind spot,' accepting any idea contrary to their racial or ethnic exceptionalism is an assault on their self-worth (Cherry, 2018). Therefore, the mere possibility of experiencing diversity or implicit bias training and cognitive dissonance may be perceived as an act of aggression. This act may, therefore, be met with equal or fiercer resistance. Studies of the effectiveness of diversity and implicit bias training conducted in the private sector have produced similar results as studies done in the medical sector. Private sector studies found that when trainees knew when they were likely to act upon their implicit biases and knew self-regulation techniques, they acted on their biased impulses less frequently (Bezrukova et al., 2012). The study found that participants acted on their biased impulses in spite of the self-regulation training when training participants were motivated to behave prejudicially. In these instances, participants did not want to regulate their behavior. I believe participants such as these are people who care too little about the disparate impacts of racial bias to do anything to subvert them.

Schools that seek to derail Jim Crow discipline can launch diversity and implicit bias training, but their respective districts influence their ability to sustain it. School districts must systematically, deliberately lead efforts to reduce disproportionality in discipline and make employees aware of their racial biases. Ultimately, districts should address systemic racial bias in all aspects of their organizations (Chang et al., 2019). If they do not, the districts undermine schools' efforts at this work. This work is social justice work, and social justice work is challenging. The challenge is hard to meet even with districts' support. It becomes exponentially more difficult without it.

Districts' characterization of support can't be, "You do it, and we will support you in your efforts to derail Jim Crow discipline." This sort of work requires districts to take the position of, "We will all do this work together." The odds of school diversity training being successful diminish greatly when the district leadership *does not* demonstrate sustained commitment to the task. Worthwhile commitment includes changing policies that produce inequitable outcomes for diverse students. Without visible district action toward the goal of equity and inclusion for all people, the workforce may perceive a district's spoken commitment to diversity and equal educational outcomes for all students as 'lip service.'

Restorative Structures Will Not Work for All Students, and That's Okay

While schools must make an earnest effort to address the problem of putting students out of school, schools must know the limitations of their innovations. In my opinion, restorative justice is not something to be hoisted onto students who have no interest in repairing the harm their behavior caused. Restorative justice is not something one can spread like magic pixie dust. Restorative justice is not a panacea; it will not work for all students. Some students will commit harm in a community and be devoid of empathy or contrition. Expect this to happen, and don't let these instances deter implementation.

There will also be moments in a restorative justice journey when students may want to participate in a restorative justice process, but their parents disallow it. Expect this to happen too. It's okay. The model this book proposes requires families' permission for their student to participate in restorative processes. A singular, rigid approach to any behavior management system rarely works, so schools must be prepared for families' refusal to allow their students to participate in restorative justice. Sometimes a family's refusal will be for the best as school personnel will not know how a conflict between students has evolved outside of school. Sometimes, situations become extremely volatile outside of school, and keeping students separated is best for all parties involved.

Getting permission from parents or guardians increases the likelihood that restorative justice efforts will be successful. It also increases the likelihood of students' investment in restorative processes. Seeking parents and guardians' permission is a humane and productive way to ensure schools do not place an unfair expectation on victims to talk to people who harmed them. Seeking permission for restorative justice proceedings also prevents schools from unwittingly coercing those who have been harmed into accepting offenders' apologies.

Students Must See the Benefit of Participating in Restorative Structures

To increase the likelihood that restorative justice will succeed, students have to see a benefit to participating. In the restorative justice model this book proposes, participation keeps offenders plugged into the school's social and academic ecosystems. There is also a clear benefit to offenders' parents and guardians. Offenders' participation keeps them in school and prevents their parents from worrying about what their children are doing at home during out-of-school consequences.

Schools and Districts Must Be Clear in Their Restorative Responses to Egregious Behaviors

To derail Jim Crow discipline, schools must be prepared with restorative responses for students who engage in egregious behaviors, such as fighting. This restorative justice model addresses the socioemotional, relational, academic, and (to some degree) societal factors that influence students to fight each other. There is a distinctive difference between this restorative justice model and others. Students who commit egregious behaviors experience restorative therapeutic benefits, but they are not exempt from out-of-school consequences. Students who fight or engage in other unwanted behavior sometimes need help navigating the emotions and circumstances that lead them to fight or make poor choices. Guidance lessons can help students reflect on their behavior and help them make choices to steer clear of what put them at risk in the first place. This approach provides justice and support for all, including uninvolved students who lose instructional time when teachers stop class to address conflicts.

The School Board Is Essential to District-Level Efforts to Derail Jim Crow Discipline

Principals can only push am agenda of fairness and restorative practices in their schools to the degree their supervisors and districts allow. The support principals most need in these efforts is the support of their school district superintendent. Superintendents can support only to the degree their supervisors allow them. Therefore, derailing Jim Crow discipline on a whole-district level cannot happen without a school board's support and blessing. School boards have tremendous sway in ensuring the policy environment is fertile to disrupt school discipline.

The passage of the African and African-American History Law in Florida provides guidance. Florida's African and African-American History legislation was created to ensure that African and African-American history was taught in Florida schools. The legislation created fiduciary obligations and relationships among school board members, lawmakers, and superintendents. In this case, support for cultural competence was legislated (Coggins & Campbell, 2008). What the Los Angeles Unified School District did to facilitate whole-district cultural competence is also instructive. The unanimous support of the LA Unified School Board was crucial in change-making. The Board encouraged resolutions and policies that led to districtwide improvements in cultural competency. They also committed to equal educational outcomes for all students (Paz). Unanimous School Board support for such solutions and policies made the Board's position clear. It ensured their one employee, the LA Unified Superintendent, was clear on the direction the Board wanted the district to take. Unanimous board support also communicates to all employees that they support their superintendent and their efforts at leading this kind of change. School board support lets superintendents lead systemic change confidently.

Derailing Jim Crow discipline is not for the faint of heart. Addressing it will take courage. In fact, it will take guts. We all have to work together to derail Jim Crow discipline as none of us exist on an island. Our actions impact each other, like an ecosystem of schooling.

On my school leadership journey, I've angered many people for the right reasons, and I don't regret angering them. Not one bit. I'm done with students being thrown out of school for silly reasons. It must stop. Leaders must understand that doing right by children and taking steps to derail Jim Crow discipline may personally cost them a lot, but students' emotional and academic health and wellness are worth it. We don't have time to tolerate adults inside and outside of schools getting in the way of good work for children. The decision to derail Jim Crow discipline is a matter of life and death for some students and their families. We owe them our best efforts. The first principle of the National Education Association's Code of Ethics reads:

> The educator strives to help each student realize his or her potential as a worthy and effective member of society. The educator therefore works to stimulate the spirit of inquiry, the acquisition of knowledge and understanding, and the thoughtful formulation of worthy goals.
> ("Code of Ethics," 2020)

We can't do that for children who are put out of school unnecessarily for ridiculous reasons. Jim Crow discipline must be derailed.

Now, if I can shed a bit more formality in these final moments we have together. As you launch or continue your restorative justice journey, I ask you to do three things:

> "Don't be trifling when it comes to this work."
> "Undermine foolishness that results in disproportionate out-of-school consequences."
> "And always do right by children."

Note

1. Young, J. L. (2016). Access, achievement, and academic resilience: The relationship between AVID and Black student participation in advanced placement courses. *Journal of Multicultural Affairs, 1*(2), 4.

References

Allensworth, E., Sebring, L., & Hart, H. (2018, March 12). Retrieved from http://blogs.edweek.org/edweek/urban_education_reform/2018/03/how_do_principals_influence_student_achievement.html

Bayanfar, F. (2013). The effect of hidden curriculum on academic achievement of high school students. *International Research Journal of Applied and Basic Sciences, 5*(6), 671–681.

Bezrukova, K., Jehn, K. A., & Spell, C. S. (2012). Reviewing diversity training: Where we have been and where we should go. *Academy of Management Learning & Education, 11*(2), 207–227.

Burgess, D. J., Beach, M. C., & Saha, S. (2017). Mindfulness practice: A promising approach to reducing the effects of clinician implicit bias on patients. *Patient Education and Counseling, 100*(2), 372–376.

Burns, M. D., Monteith, M. J., & Parker, L. R. (2017). Training away bias: The differential effects of counterstereotype training and self-regulation on stereotype activation and application. *Journal of Experimental Social Psychology, 73*, 97–110.

Chang, E., Milkman, K., Zarrow, L., Brabaw, K., Grommet, D., Rebele, R., . . . Grant, A. (2019, July 9). *Does diversity training work the way it's supposed to?* Retrieved from https://hbr.org/2019/07/does-diversity-training-work-the-way-its-supposed-to

Cherry, K. (2018, Fecruary 22). *Bias blind spot: Are you blind to your own biases?* Retrieved from www.explorepsychology.com/bias-blind-spot/

Code of ethics. (2020, September 14). Retrieved from www.nea.org/resource-library/code-ethics

Coggins, P., & Campbell, S. D. (2008). Using cultural competence to close the achievement gap. *The Journal of Pan African Studies, 2*(4), 44–59.

Department of justice announces new department-wide implicit bias training for personnel. (2016). Retrieved from www.justice.gov/opa/pr/department-justice-announces-new-department-wide-implicit-bias-training-personnel

Fritscher, L. (2019, April 12). *Therapeutic role-playing for phobia treatment.* Retrieved from www.verywellmind.com/therapeutic-role-playing-2671644

Paz, S. *Cultural competency.* Retrieved from www.aasa.org/schooladministrator article.aspx?id=4096

Young, J. L. (2016). Access, achievement, and academic resilience: The relationship between AVID and Black student participation in advanced placement courses. *Journal of Multicultural Affairs, 1*(2), Article 4.

Acknowledgements

Regina James is an amazing school counselor and restorative justice professional. She is a natural at this work. Even the initials of her name are RJ. The restorative justice work she is doing in Nevada is amazing. I have never met a more powerful advocate for children than the "incomparable" Ms. Regina James. Her command of the policy, practice, and history associated with restorative justice is incredible. I am so thankful to know Regina and to call her my colleague and friend. I predict her dissertation about restorative practices will change the game and help many people. I can't wait to read it when it's done.

Gerald Robinson is the preeminent school social worker and a fantastic restorative justice practitioner. He is graceful, kind, and compassionate. Gerald can comfort and calm people in their toughest moments, which is key when facilitating restorative justice proceedings. He's so good at getting people to reflect on moments in their lives; it appears effortless. When he speaks, the room listens because he speaks from his heart and soul. The positive energy Gerald brings to this work is uplifting. I am thankful to call Gerald my colleague and friend. I appreciate his help during this restorative justice journey.

Claire Ince is an amazing writer I was in a writer's workshop with at Howard University. I wanted this book to communicate complex ideas, but not be overly academic. I wanted the ideas rooted in narrative. But my narrative writing was rusty. I needed to recapture my "old Zac Robbins voice." Claire helped me do that. Claire and I hadn't talked in years, but it was like time had stood still when we started working. We reviewed each other's writing, as we did when we were undergrads. It was absolutely wonderful. Claire is the best. I am deeply thankful to call Claire my friend.

Dr. Marjorie Conner is one of the first people I met when I moved to Nevada. We became friends. Now we are more like family. Dr. Conner was there when we launched restorative justice. She was also there for me as I was formulating and fine-tuning my thoughts for this book. I appreciate Marjorie very much. I am thankful for Marjorie's feedback, insight, and for being an amazing person and resource for educators around the country.

You would not be reading this book if it were not for the guidance I received from Dr. William Smith, Chair of the Department of Education, Culture, and Society at the University of Utah. When I had a moment of doubt about my manuscript, Dr. Smith got my mind right. He said, "Send your manuscript to publishers. Get it out there!" The rest is history. Thank you, Dr. Smith. Friendship is essential to the soul.

Jemma Galindo provided amazing feedback on my manuscript. I shared my ideas with Jemma when my manuscript was in its rawest form. She is a wizard with words. I believe Jemma is Australia's eighth natural wonder and a true gem. I am appreciative of Jemma's help with this book and for believing in restorative practices.